TOUCHLESS AUTOMATIC WONDER

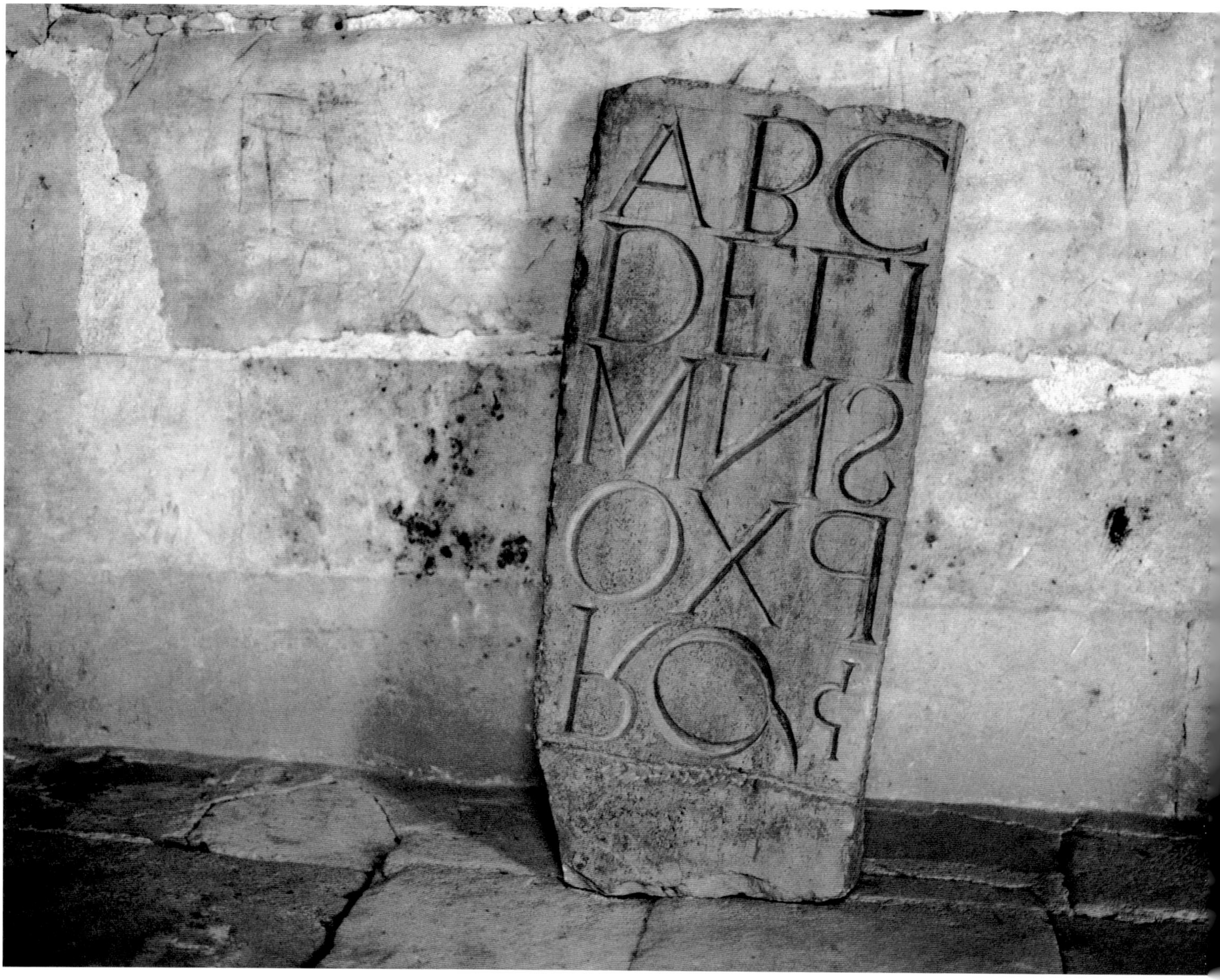
ABC

TOUCHLESS AUTOMATIC WONDER

found text from the real world

photographs by LEWIS KOCH

Borderland Books

for Leona Rostenberg & Madeleine B. Stern

their shared life in books and their dedication to the variousness of words
remain a source of inspiration and wonder

Wonder is a measure of what this world is all about. Not that wonder can be measured because it can't. Yet, in its own inexplicable way, it can be an antidote to the chaos of the world.

My initial impulse to make photographs was, I suppose, as Garry Winogrand said, *to see what things look like photographed.* Somewhat later on I came to understand that the obsession was not just this one thing, but many. A desire to follow an abiding sense of curiosity, to allow for the possibilities of digression, to experience the immediacy of the everyday, and through this, on the most elemental level, simply, to wonder.

Memory plays an essential role here as well. Photographs remain as a residue of memory. They are fragments of experience, conjecture and awe, a sometimes deliberate, sometimes accidental account of one's life. In some ways they actually are memory. I often think of photographs as my paper memory.

I like seeing things and I like words. There is something revelatory about the two together, an almost pentecostal feeling of seeing in tongues. Signs and symbols and scraps of text are ubiquitous in our daily lives, and can be read, like dreams, for their various meanings or they can be accepted, more poetically, as unfathomable koans.
I prefer to read them as both. Like the photographs in this book.

Lewis Koch
Madison, Wisconsin
June, 2009

Ce n'était ni vrai ni faux, c'était vécu.
(It was neither true nor false, but what was experienced.)

ANDRÉ MALRAUX, *La Condition Humaine*

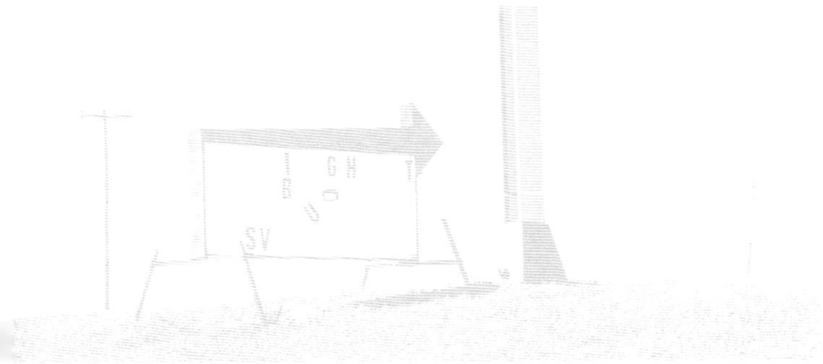

Something strange is creeping across me.
La Celestina has only to warble the first few bars
Of "I Thought about You" or something mellow from
Amadigi di Gaula for everything—a mint condition can
Of Rumford's Baking Powder, a celluloid earring, Speedy
Gonzales, the latest from Helen Topping Miller's fertile
Escritoire, a sheaf of suggestive pix on greige, deckle-edged
Stock—to come clattering through...

JOHN ASHBERY, *Daffy Duck in Hollywood*

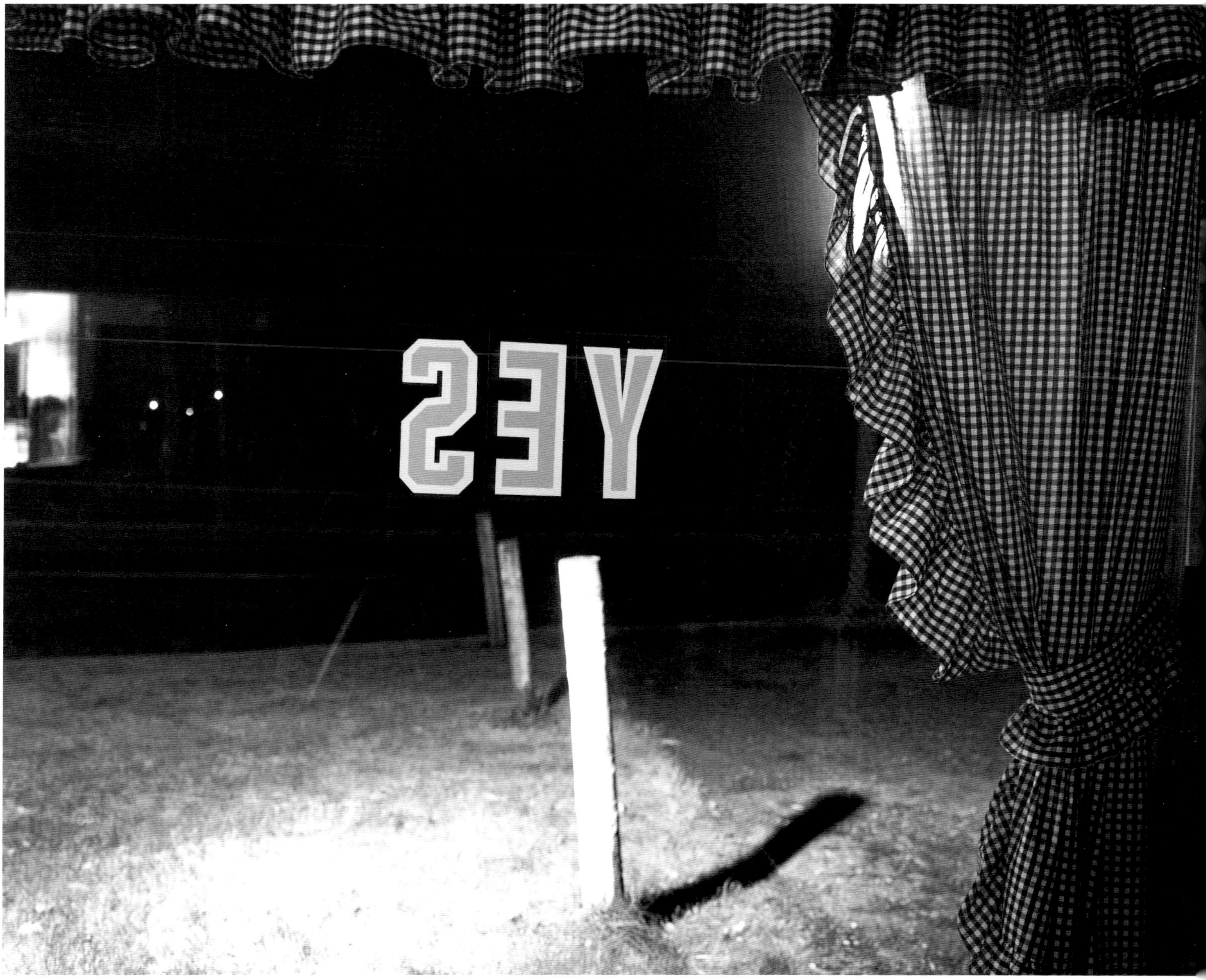
YES

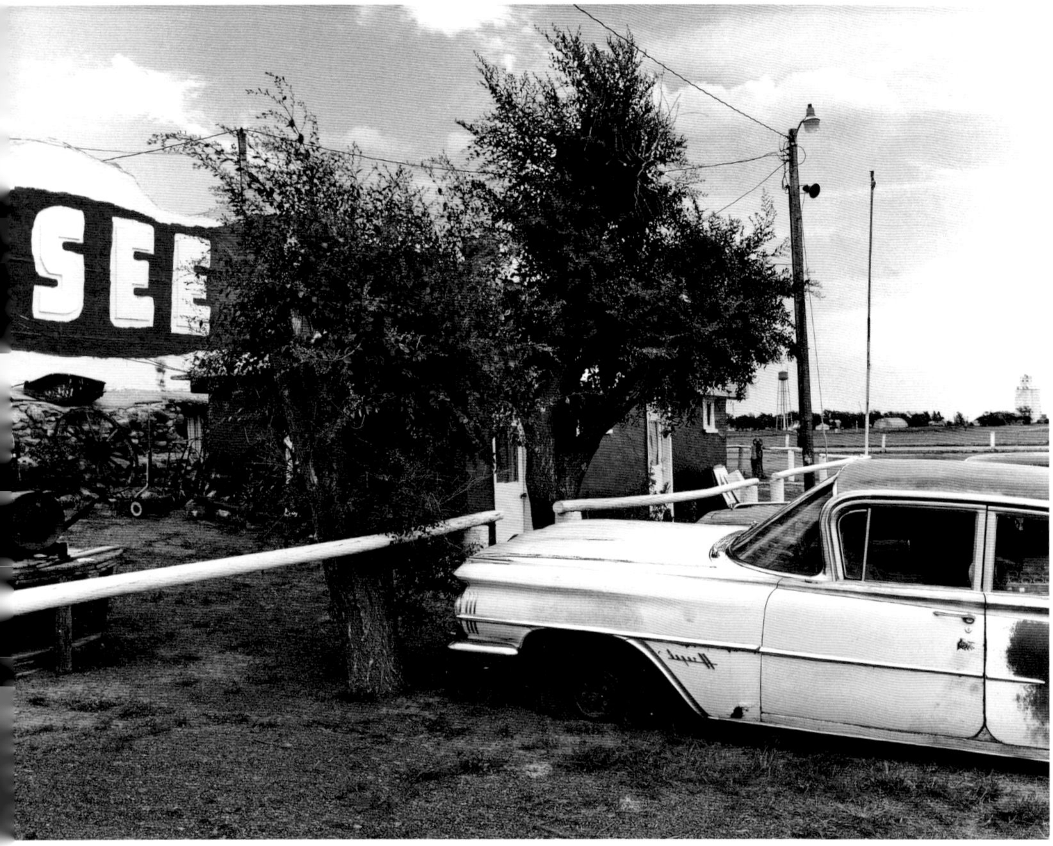
SEE

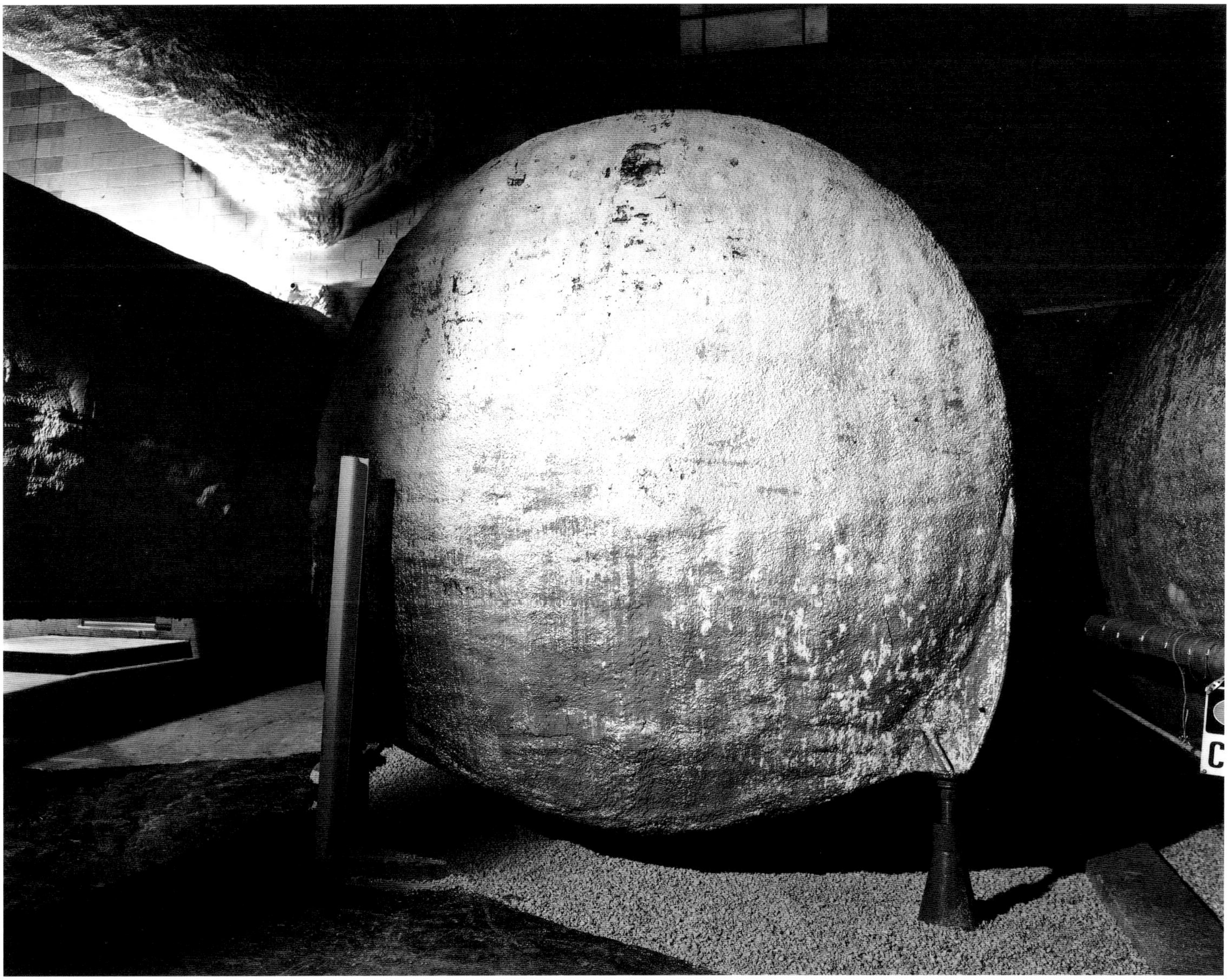

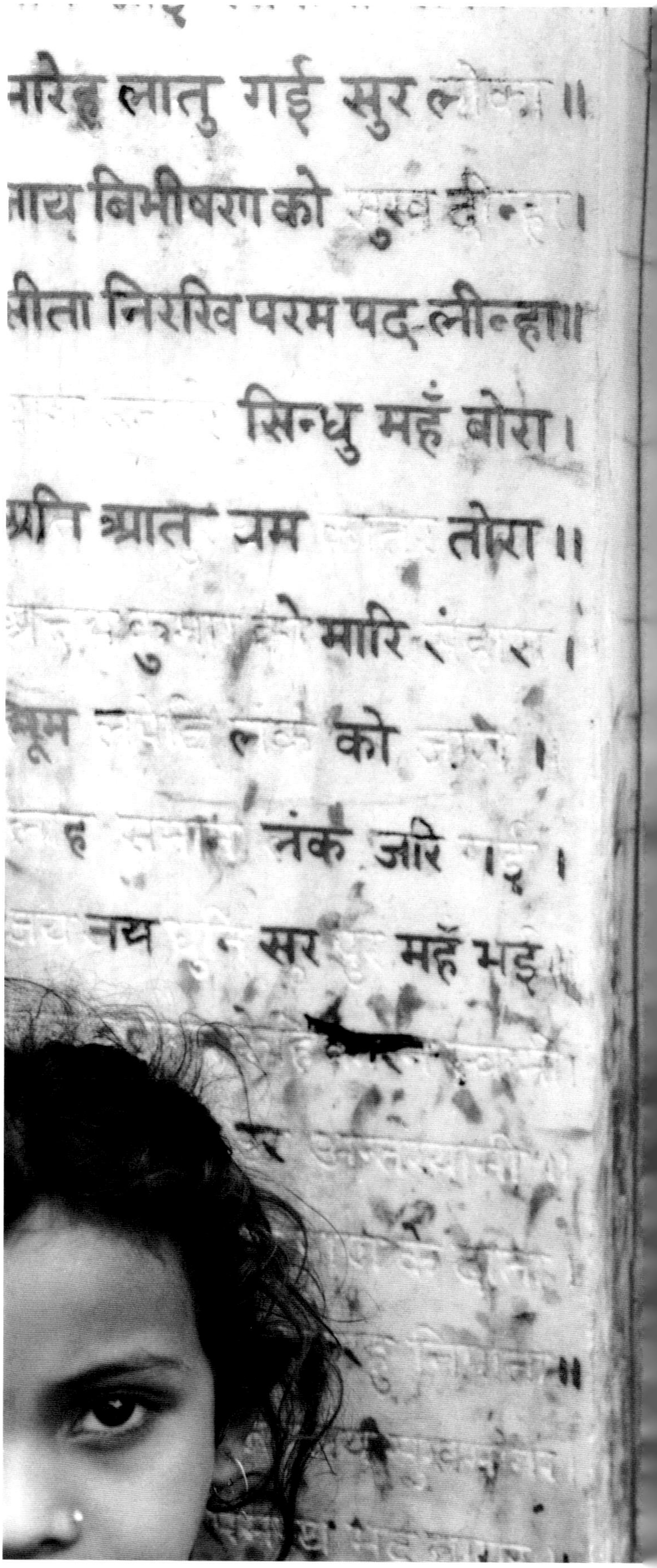
लातु गई सुर
बिभीषरण को
निरखि परम पद
सिन्धु महँ बोरा।
तोरा ॥
मारि
को
जरि
सर
महँ

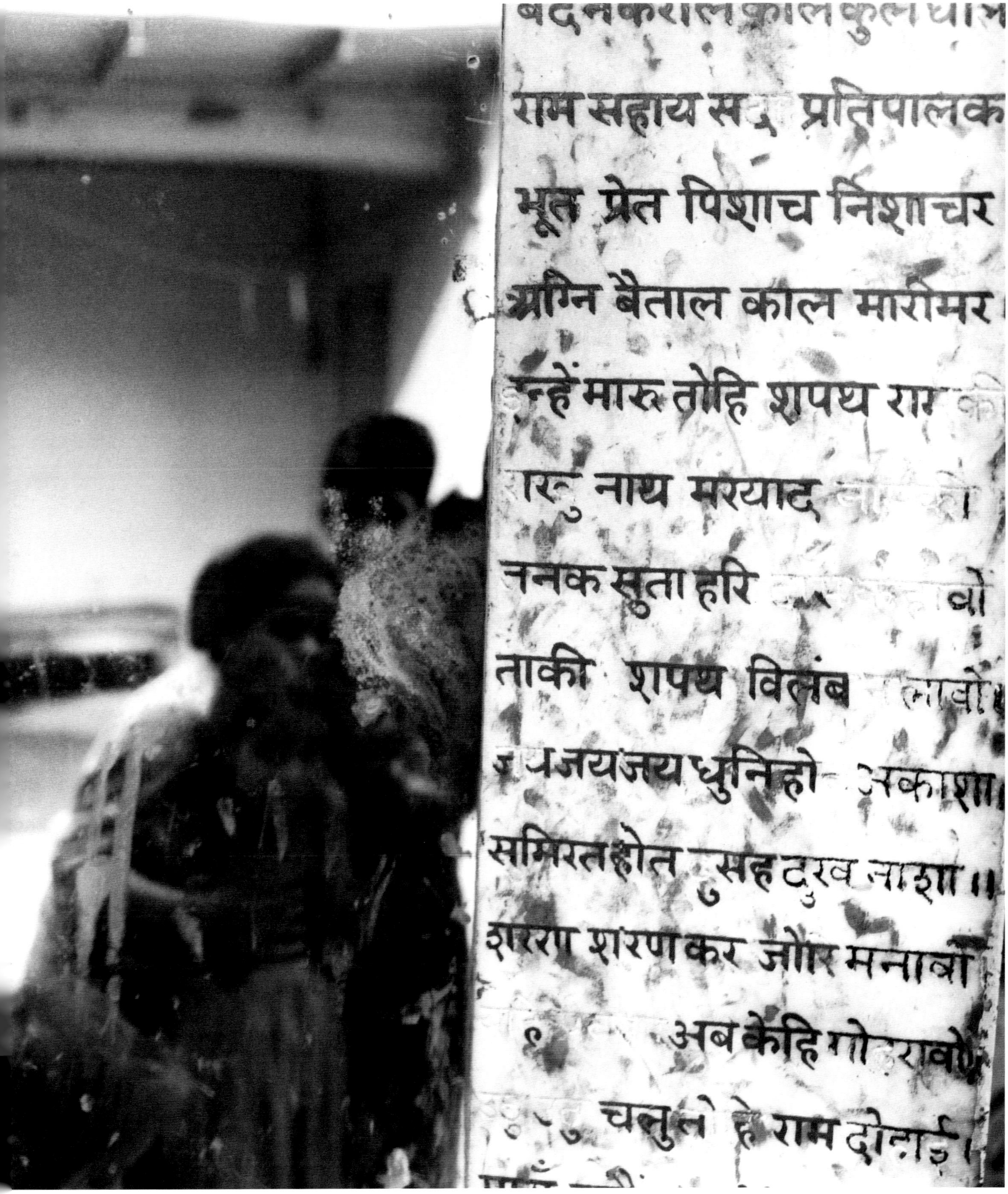

भूत प्रेत पिशाच निशाचर
अग्नि बैताल काल मारीमर
मारु तोहि शपथ
नाथ मरयाद
सुता हरि
ताकी शपथ विलंब
जयजय धुनि हो
शरण शरण कर जोर मनावौ
अब केहि
हे राम दोहाई

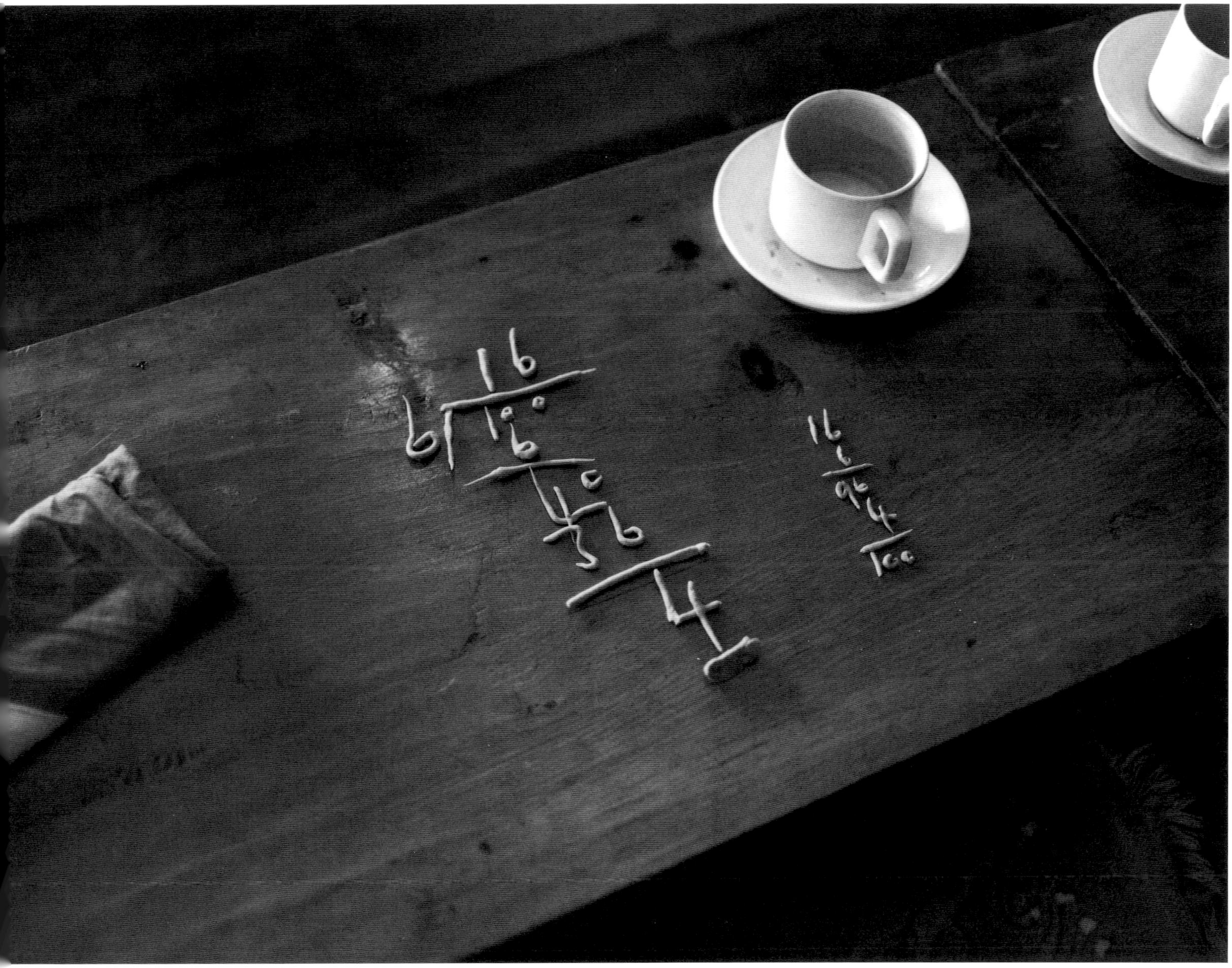

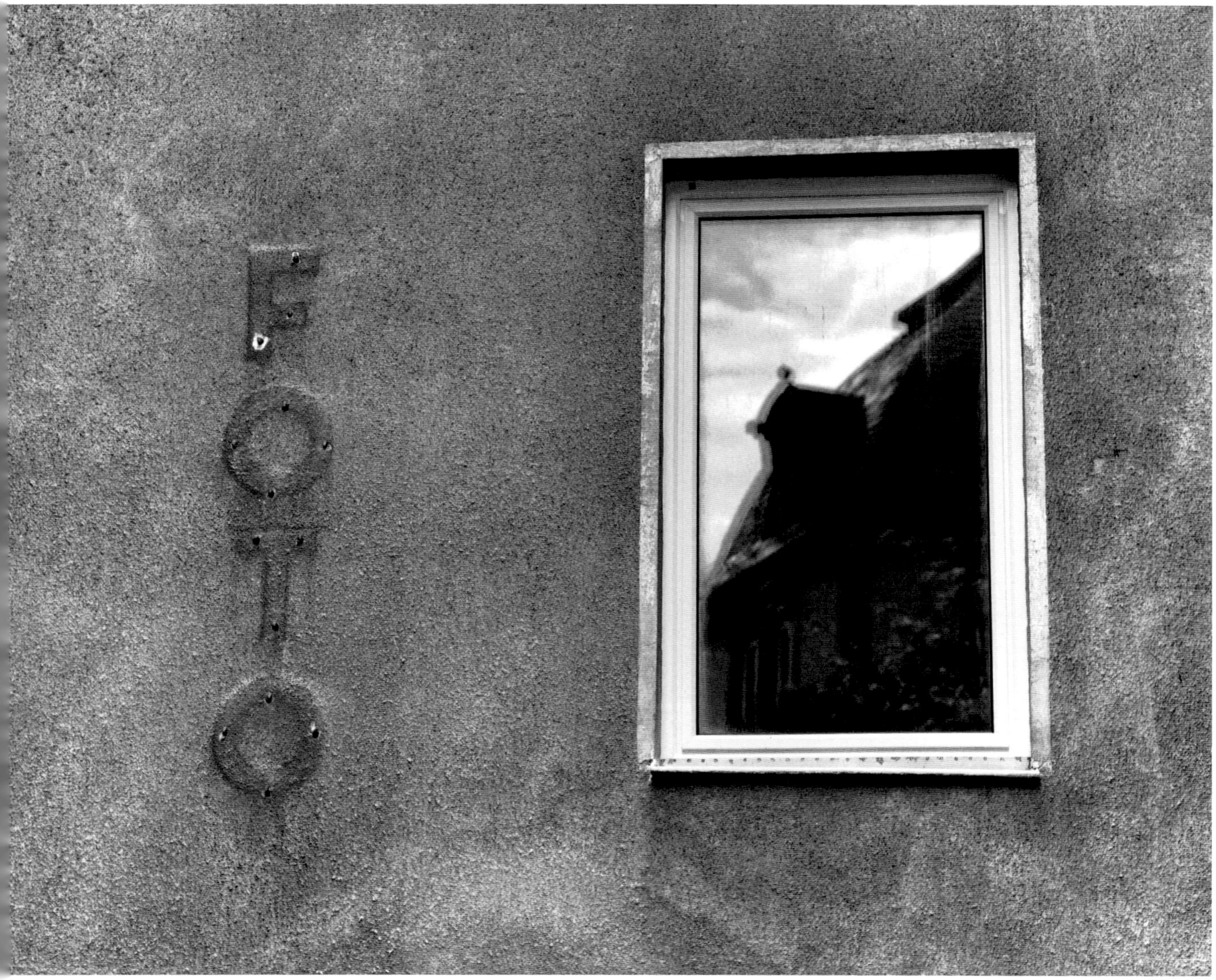
FOTO

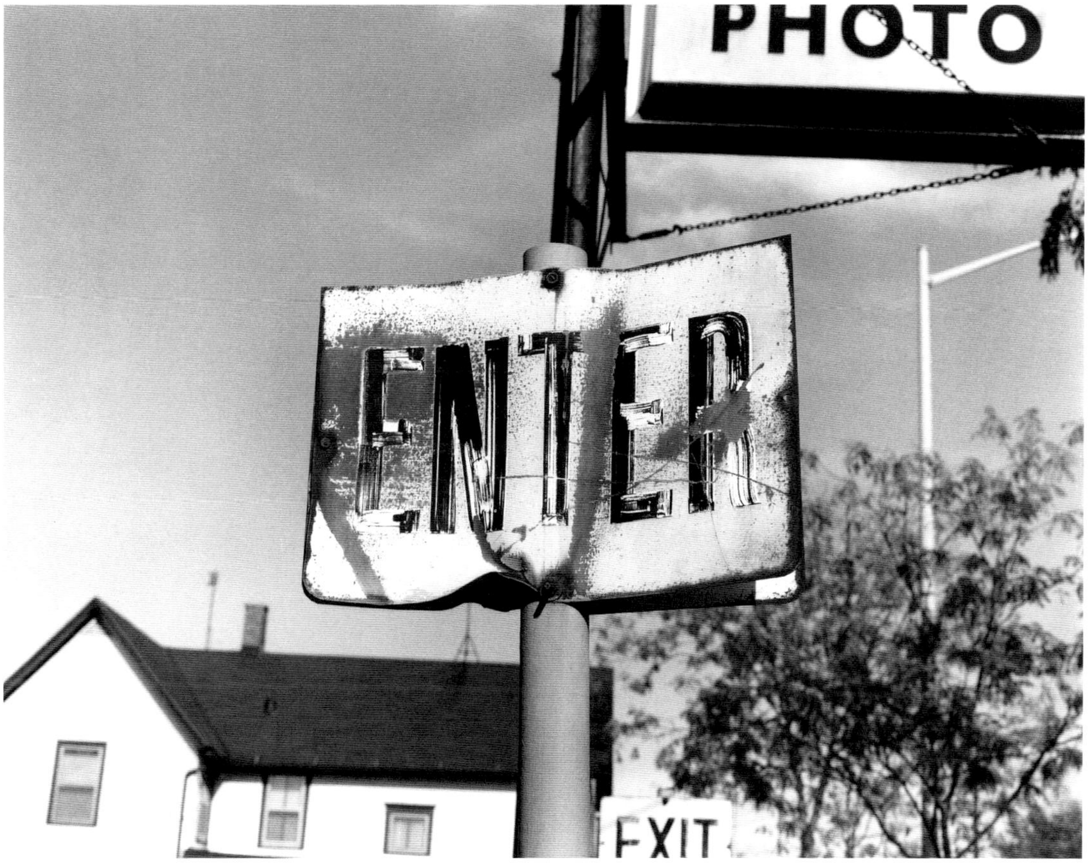
PHOTO
ENTER
EXIT

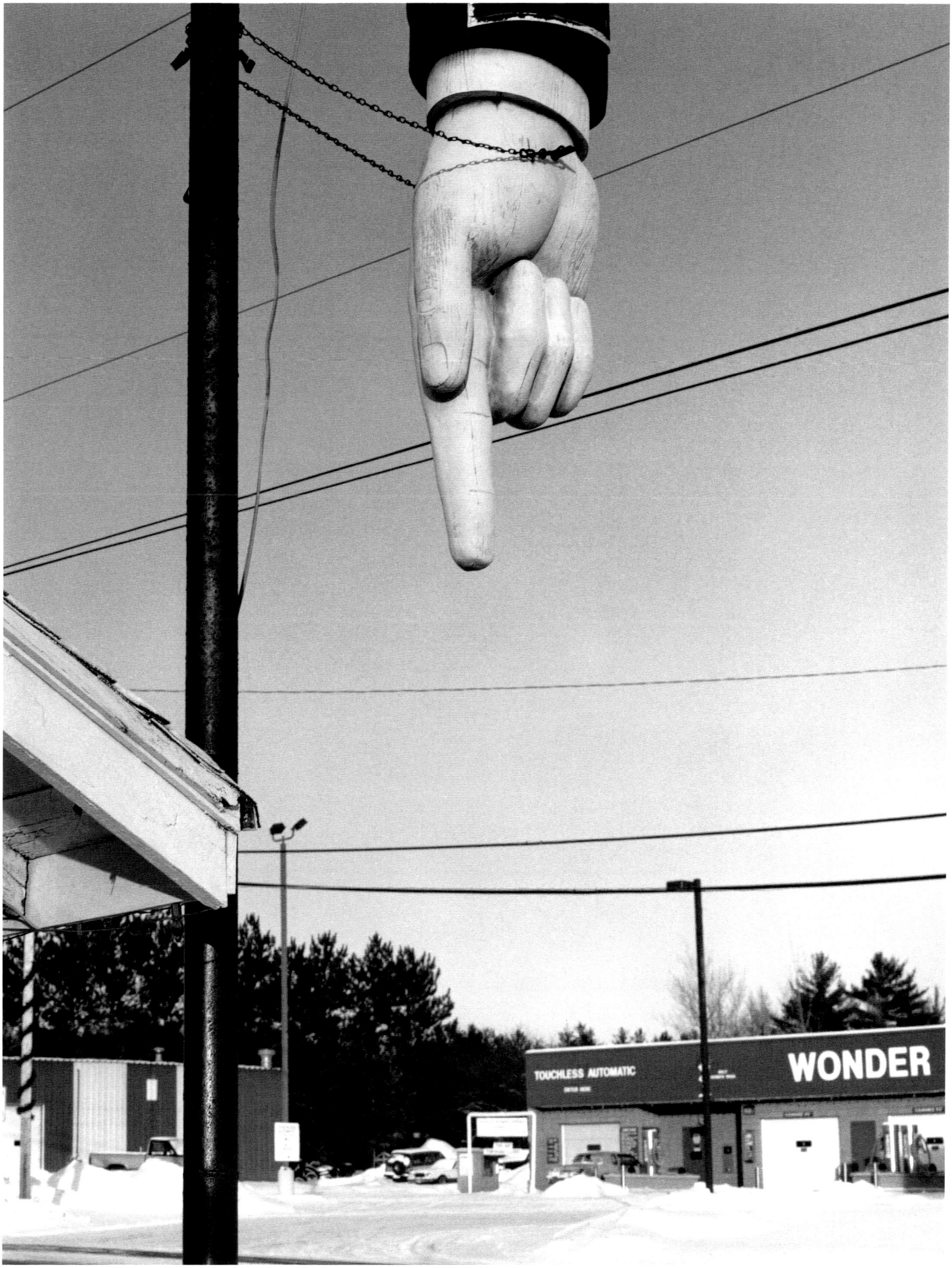
TOUCHLESS AUTOMATIC
WONDER

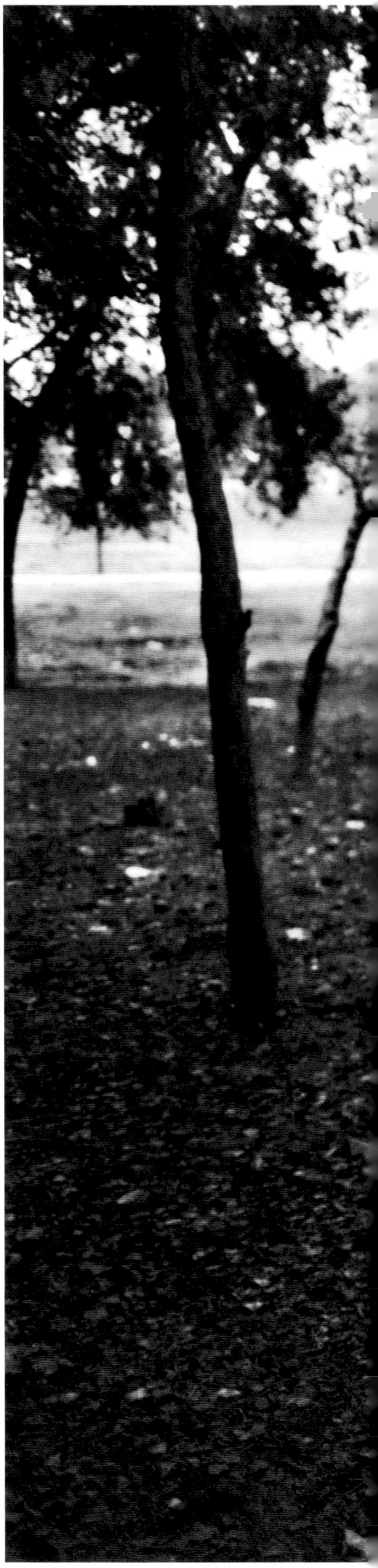

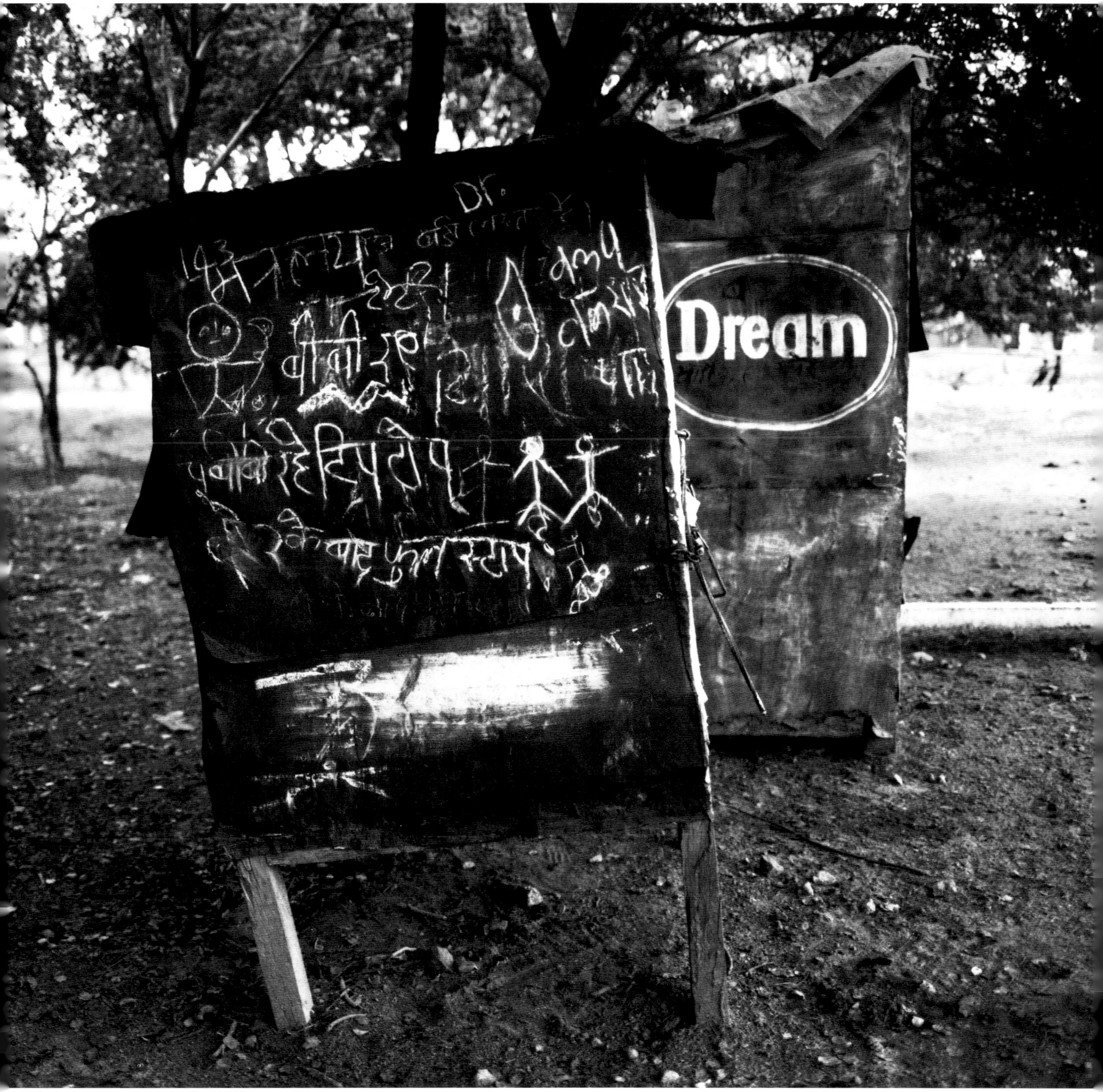
Dr.
Dream

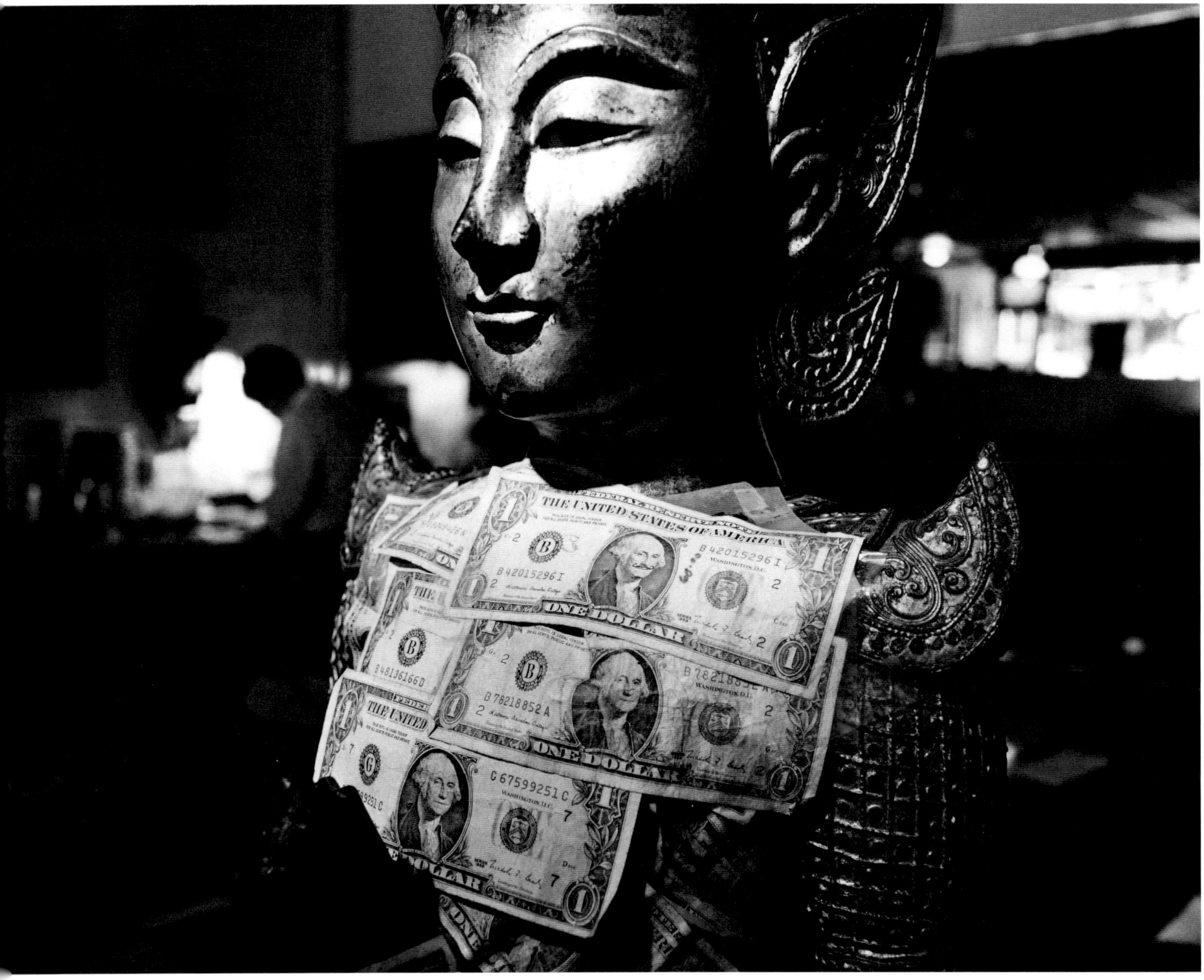
THE UNITED STATES OF AMERICA
B42015296I
WASHINGTON, D.C.
ONE DOLLAR
B78218852A
C67599251C
WASHINGTON, D.C.
ONE DOLLAR

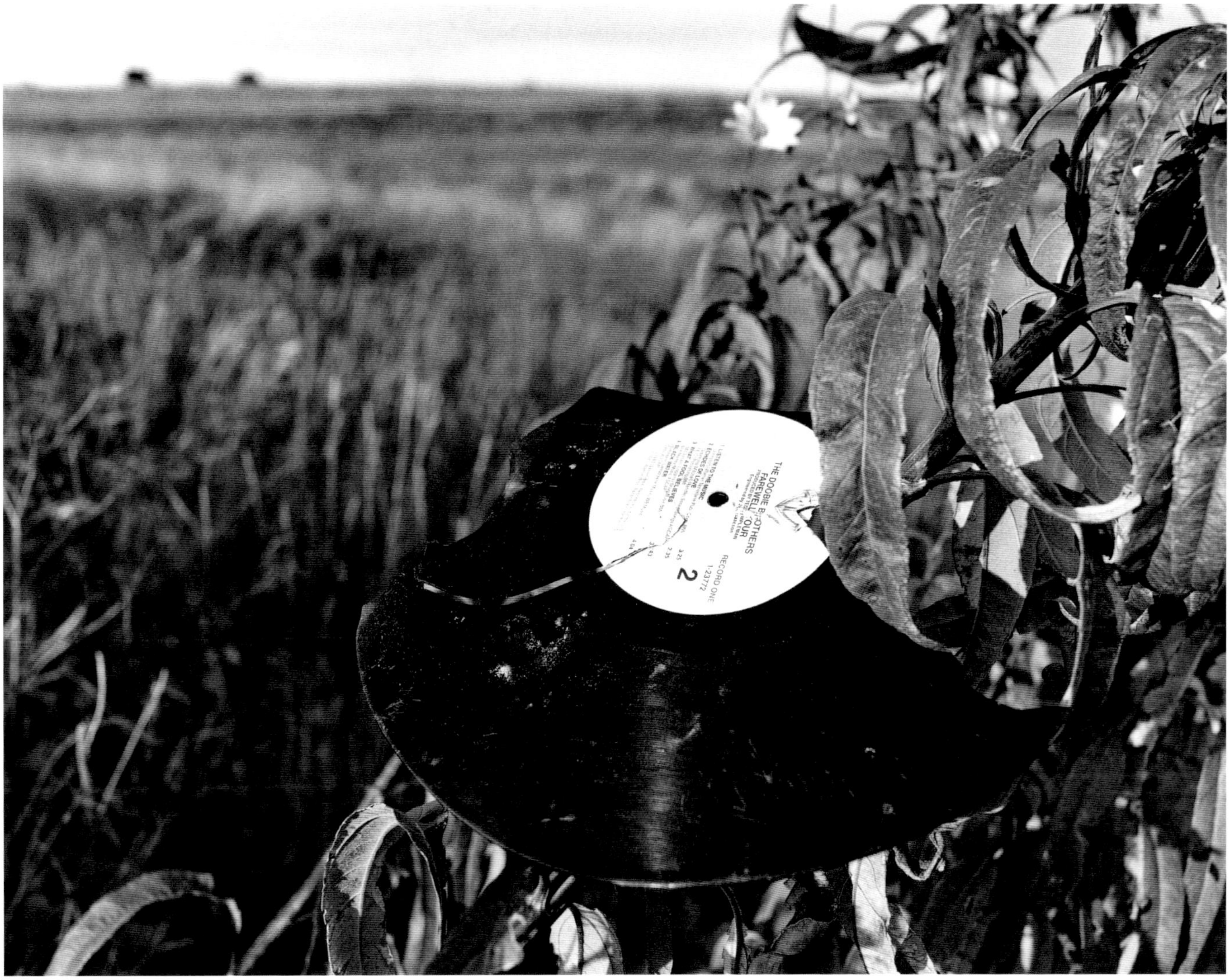
RECORD ONE
2

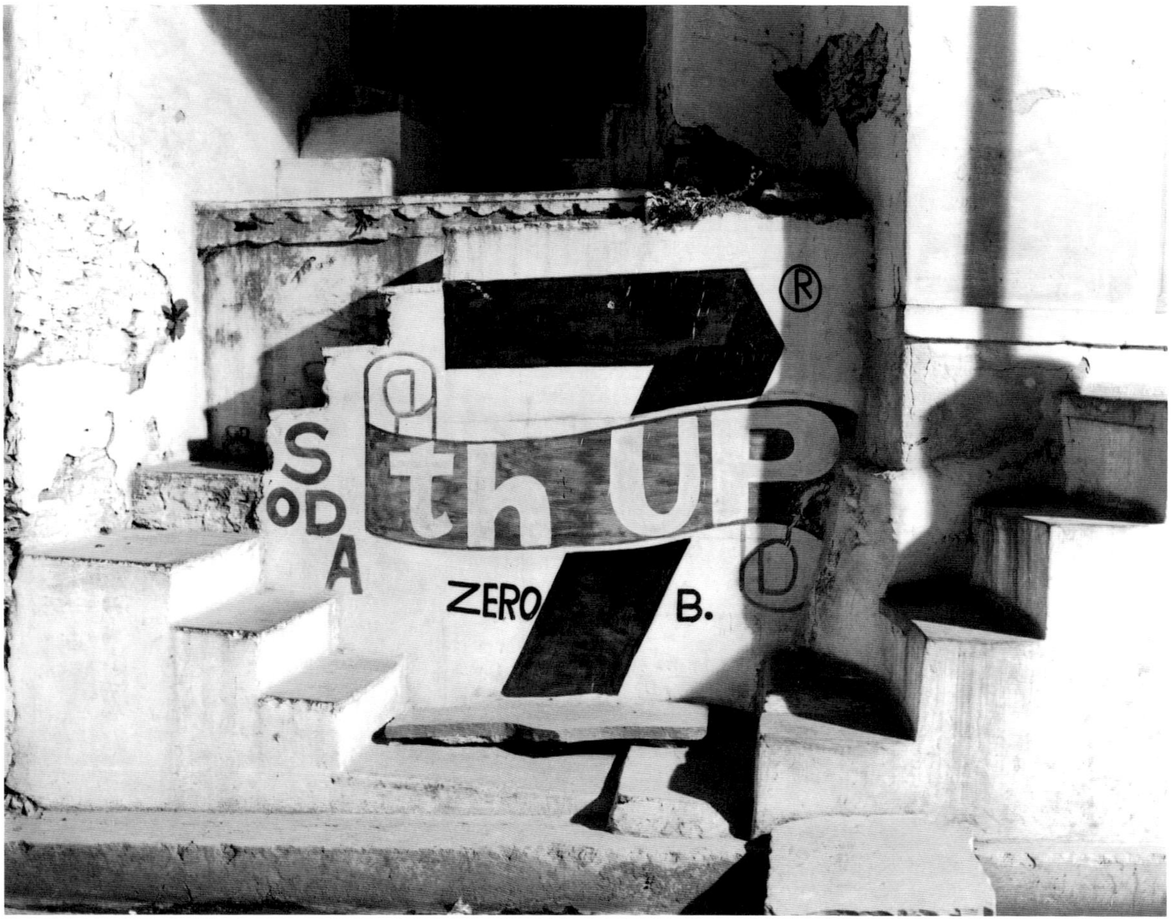

SODA
th UP
ZERO B.

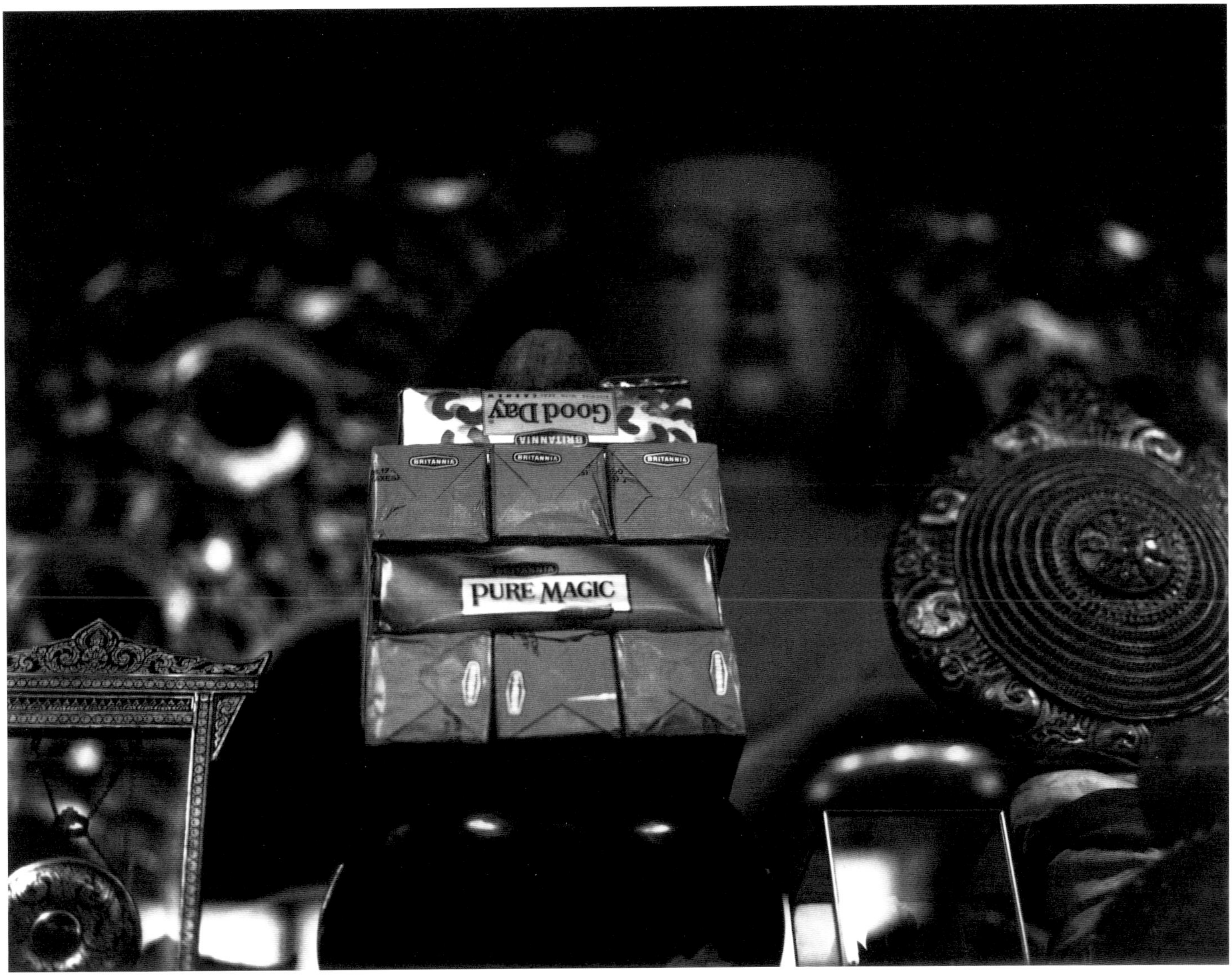
Good Day
BRITANNIA
BRITANNIA
BRITANNIA
BRITANNIA
PURE MAGIC

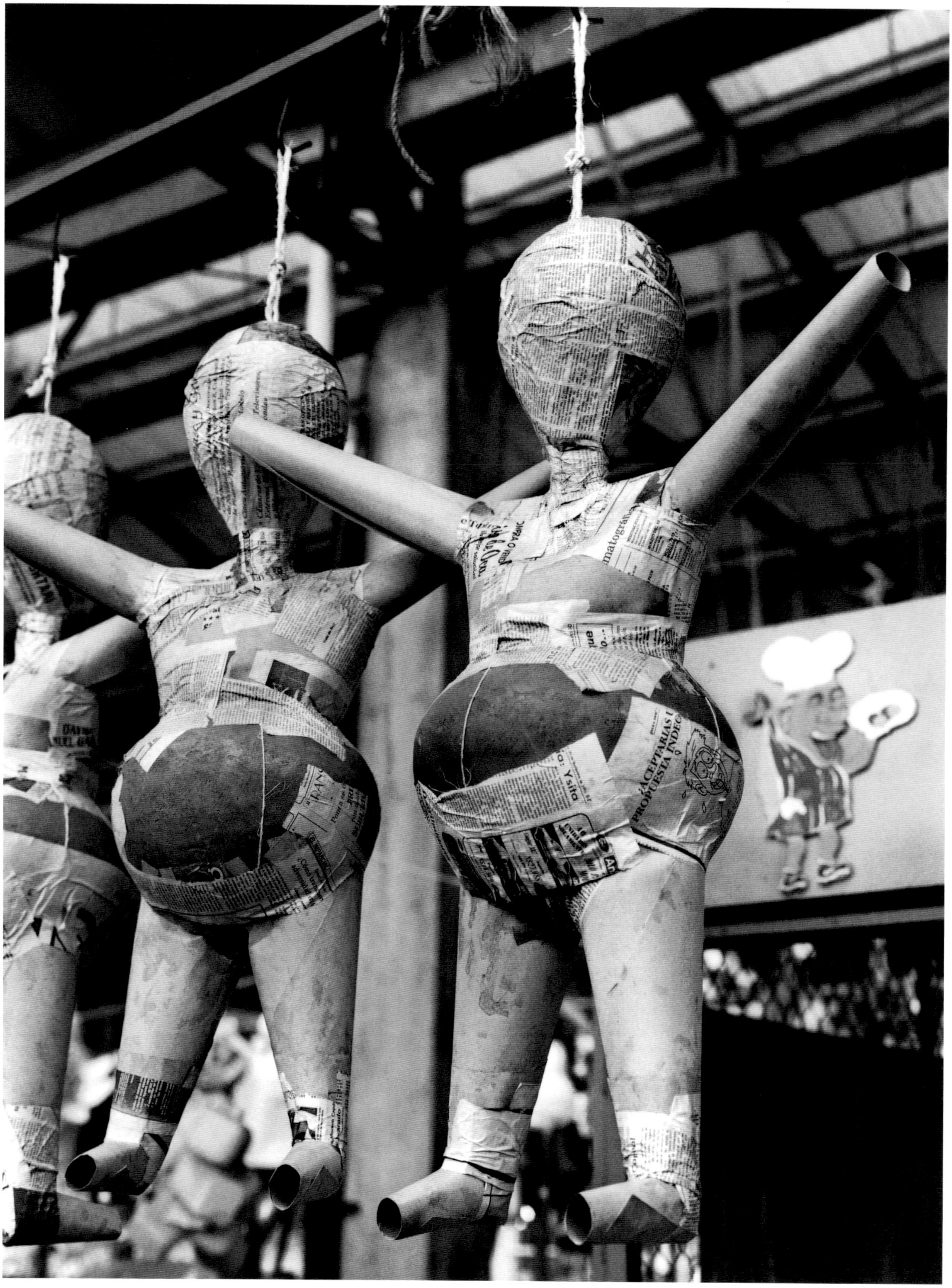

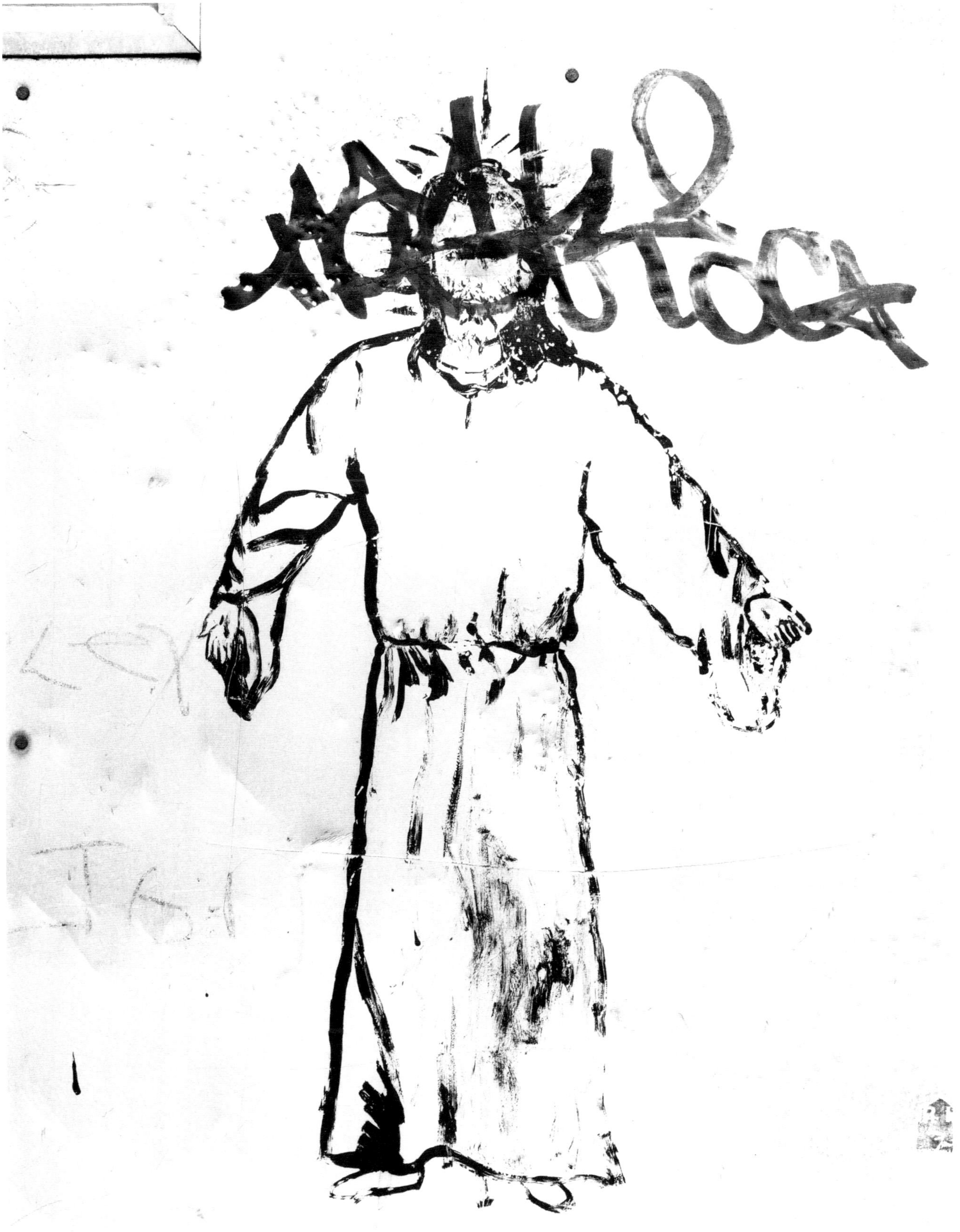

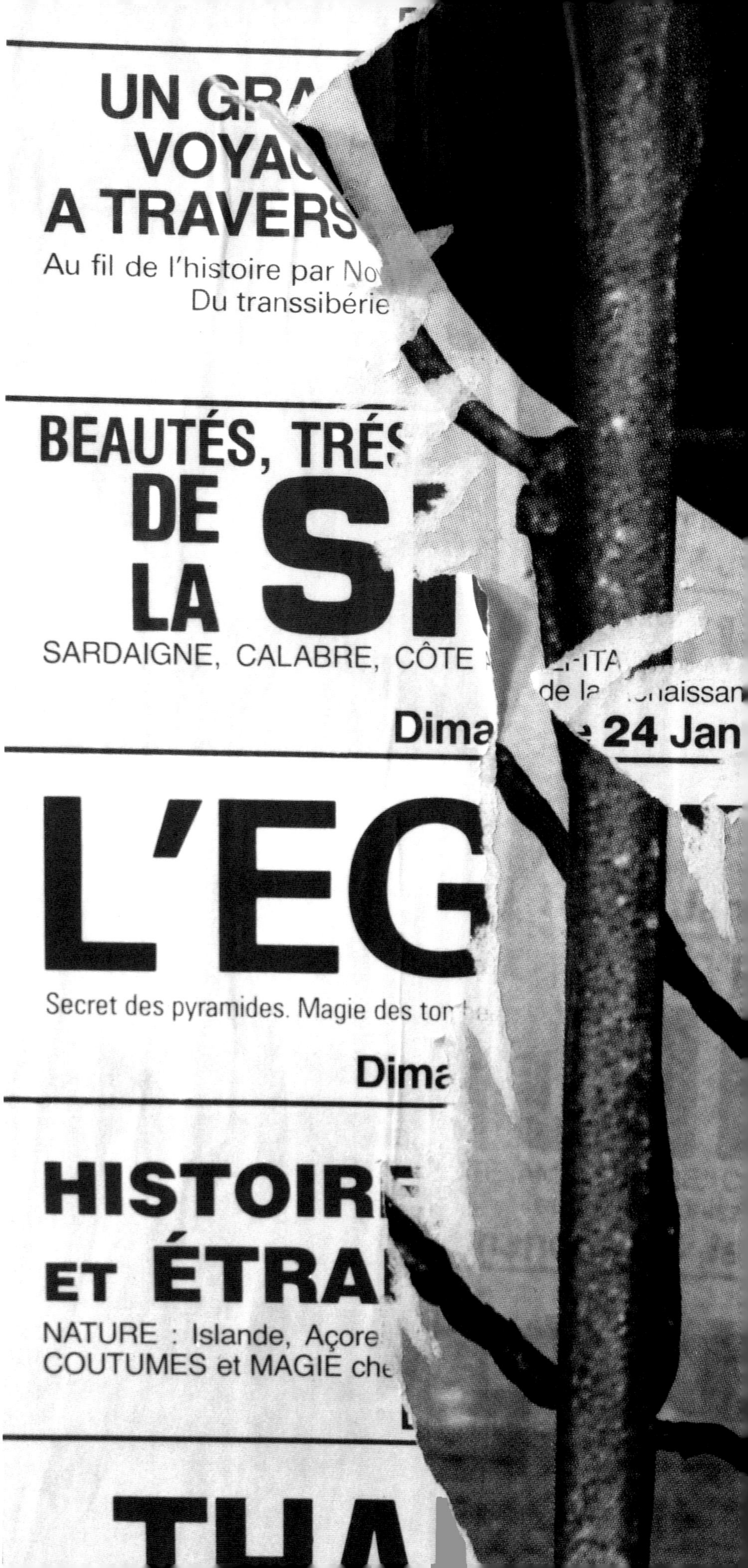
UN GRA
VOYAG
A TRAVERS
Au fil de l'histoire par No
Du transsibérie
BEAUTÉS, TRÉS
DE
LA S
SARDAIGNE, CALABRE, CÔTE
de la
Dima
24 Jan
L'EG
Secret des pyramides. Magie des tor
Dima
HISTOIR
ET ÉTRA
NATURE : Islande, Açore
COUTUMES et MAGIE che
THA

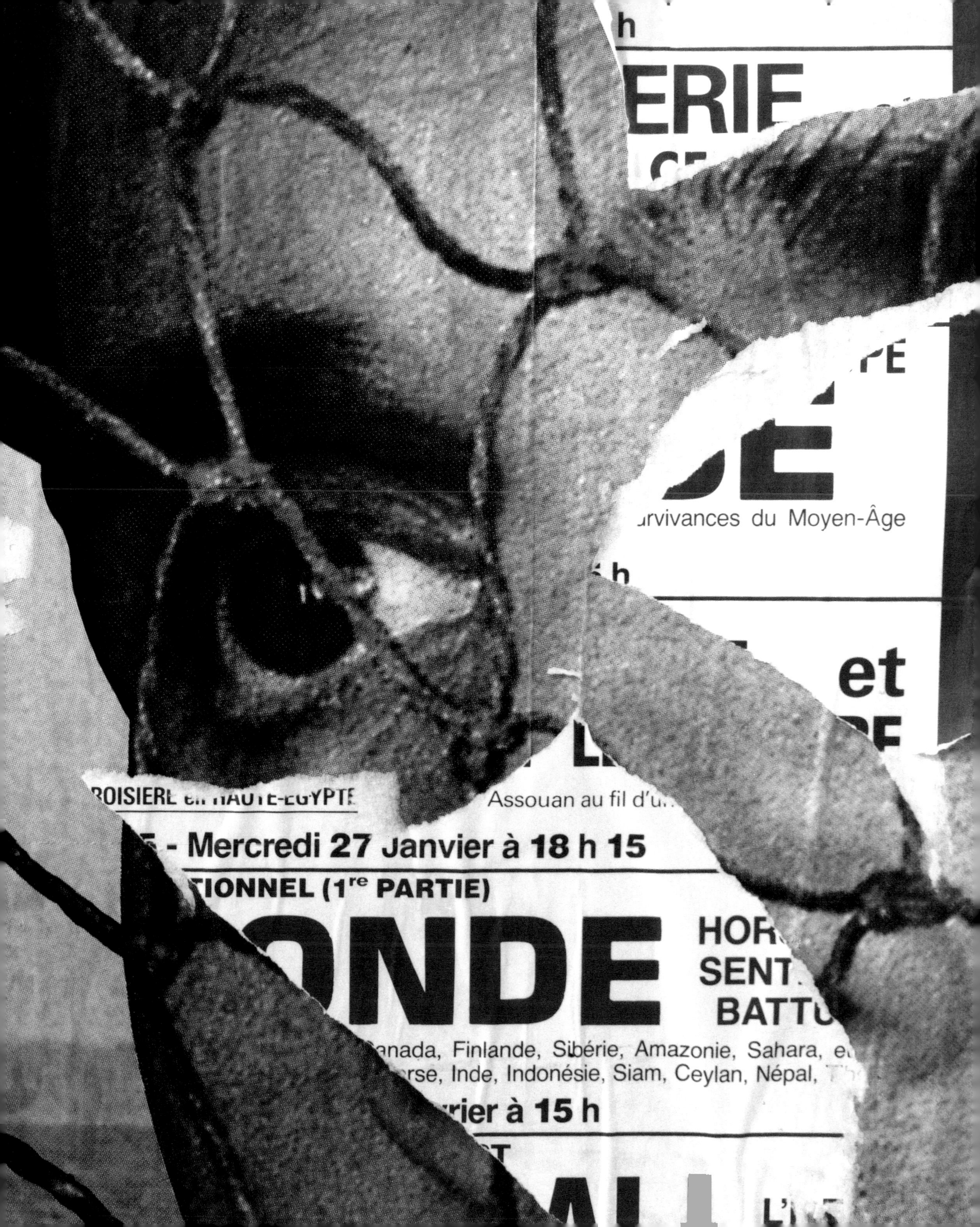

ERIE
PE
urvivances du Moyen-Âge
et
ROISIERE
Assouan au fil d'u
- Mercredi 27 Janvier à 18 h 15
TIONNEL (1re PARTIE)
ONDE
HOR
SENT
BATT
Canada, Finlande, Sibérie, Amazonie, Sahara,
rse, Inde, Indonésie, Siam, Ceylan, Népal,
rier à 15 h

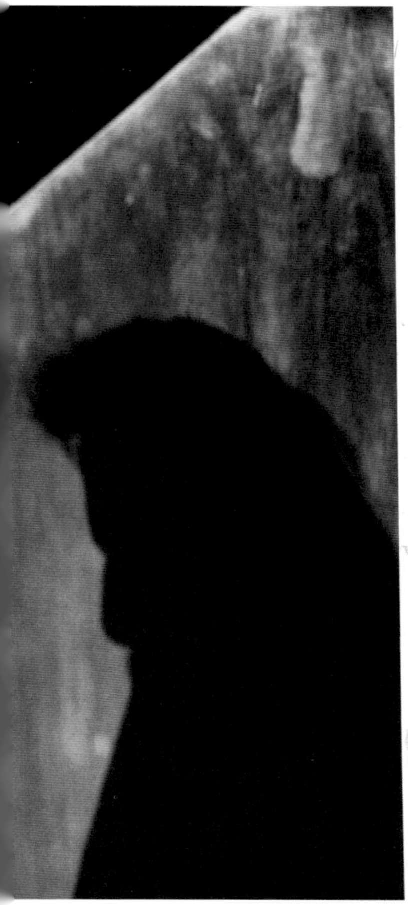

JOE
FUCK
DON

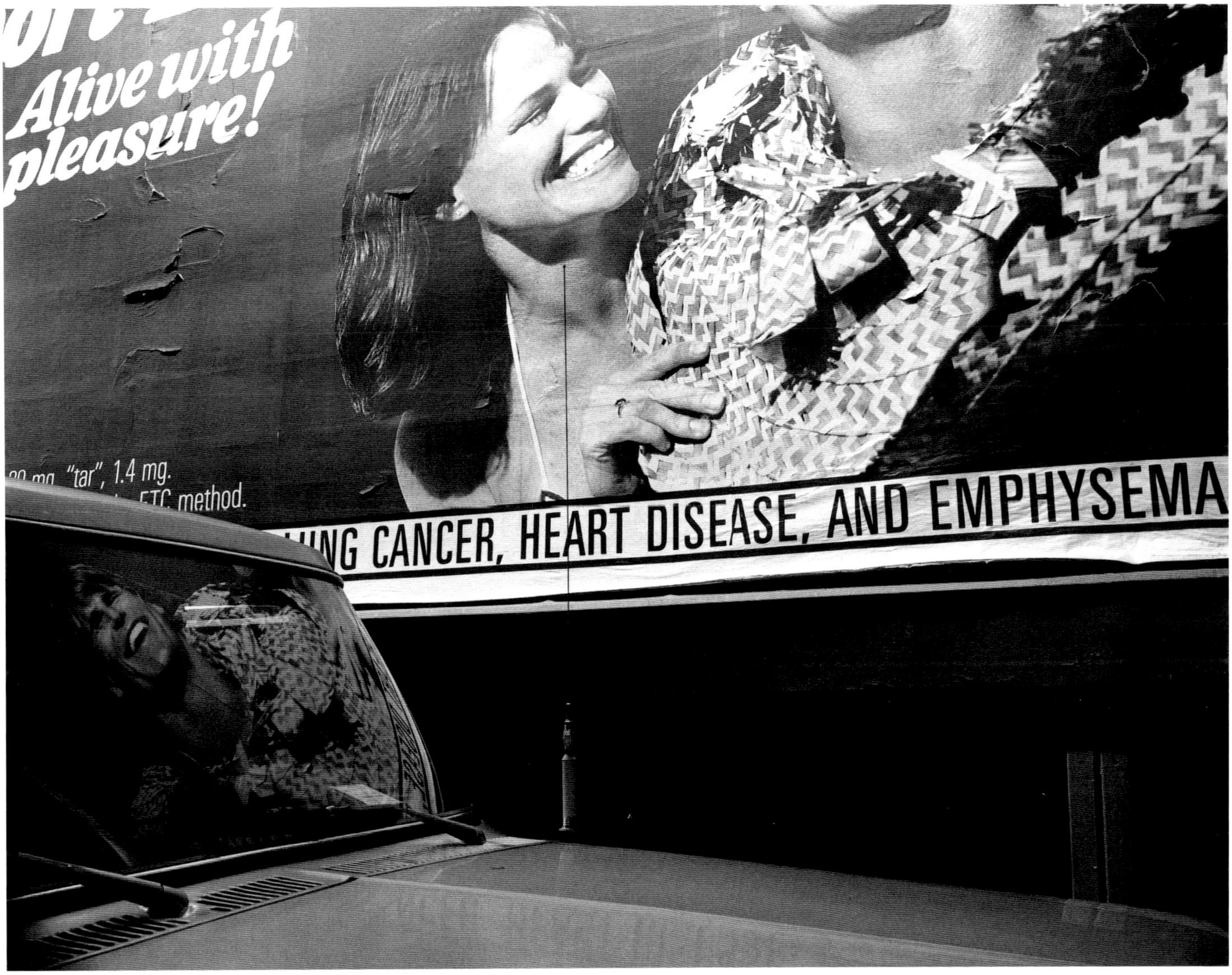
Alive with pleasure!
"tar", 1.4 mg.
FTC method.
CANCER, HEART DISEASE, AND EMPHYSEMA

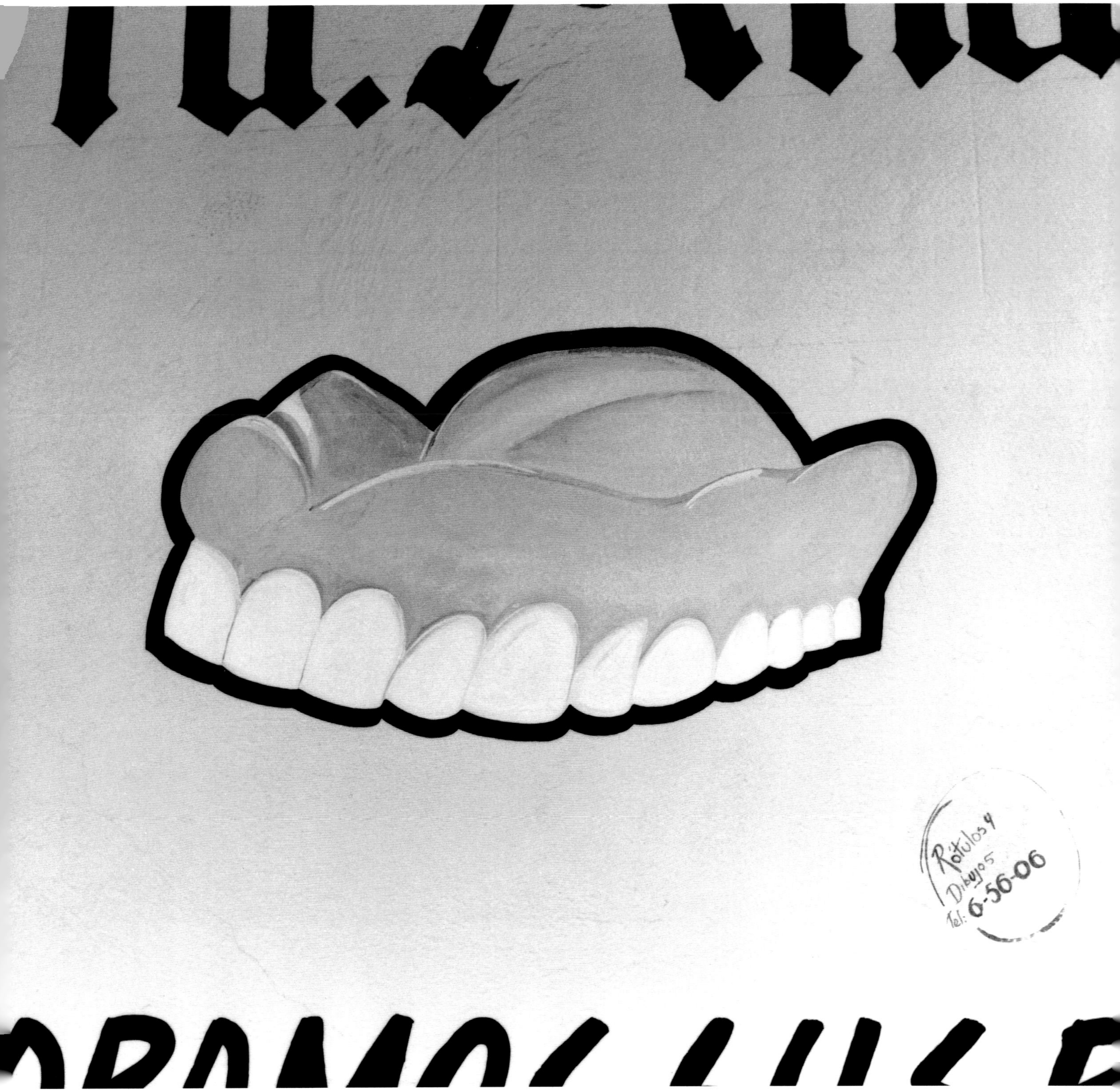
Rótulos y
Dibujos
Tel: 6-56-06

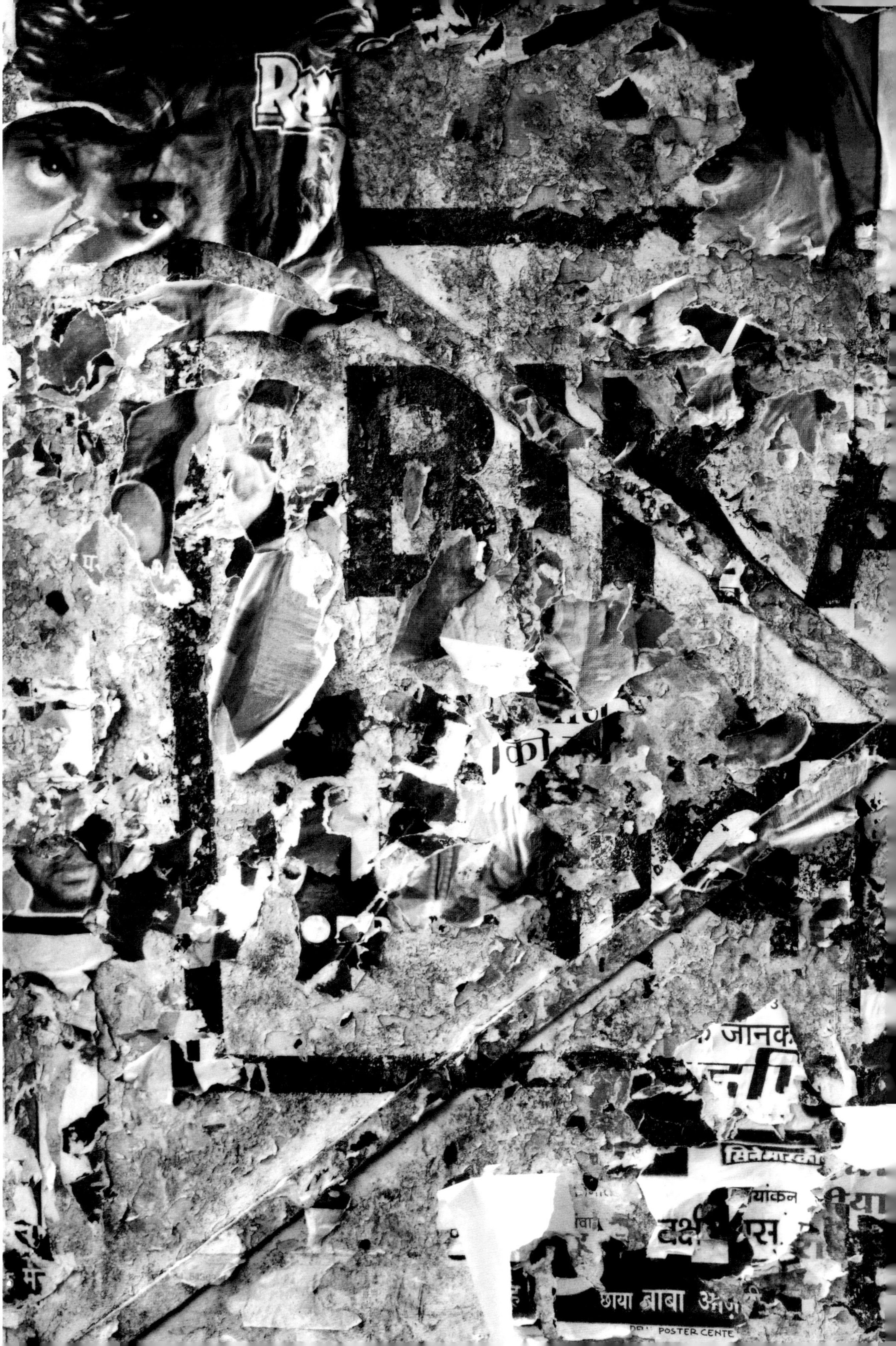
छाया बाबा
POSTER CENTE

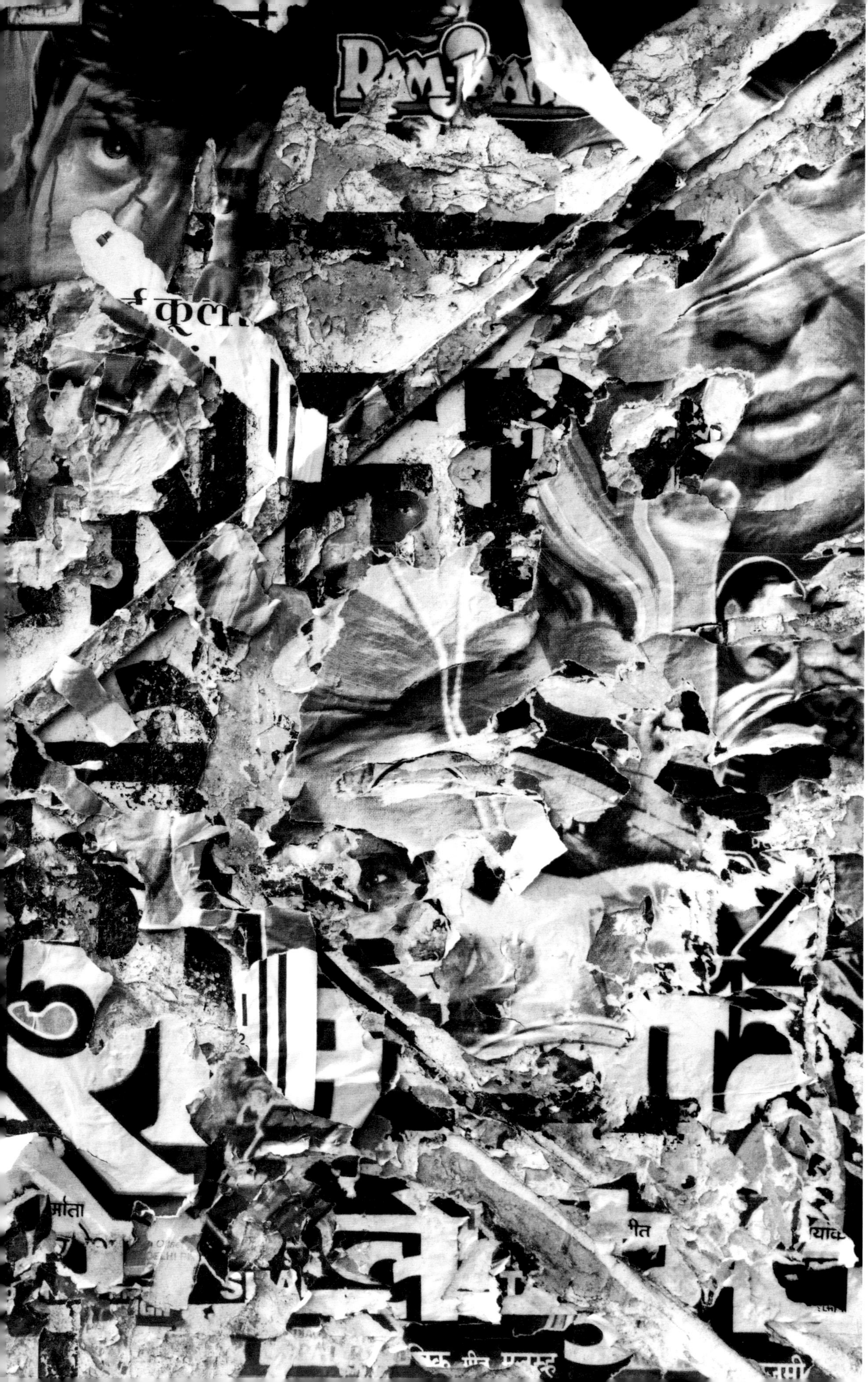

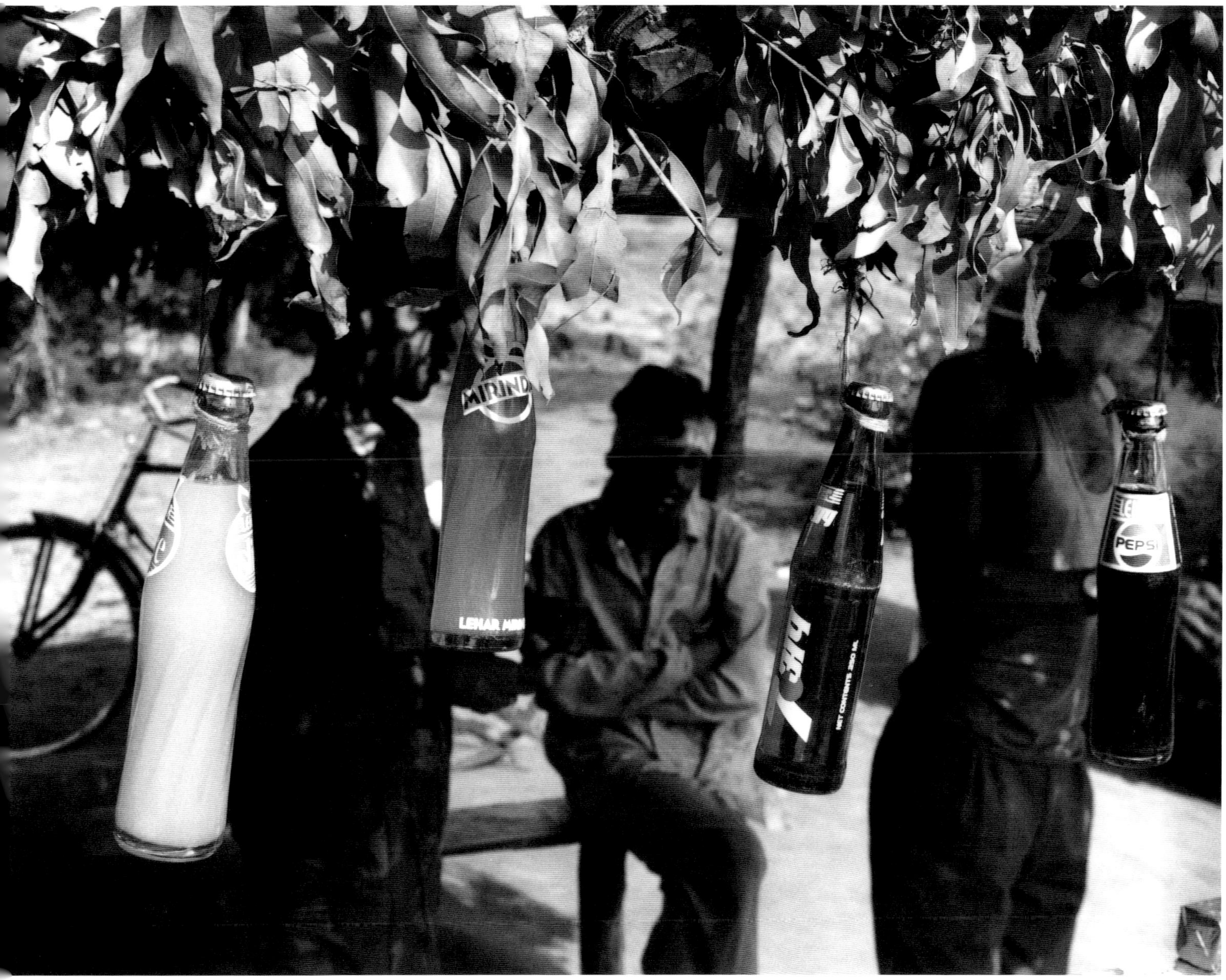

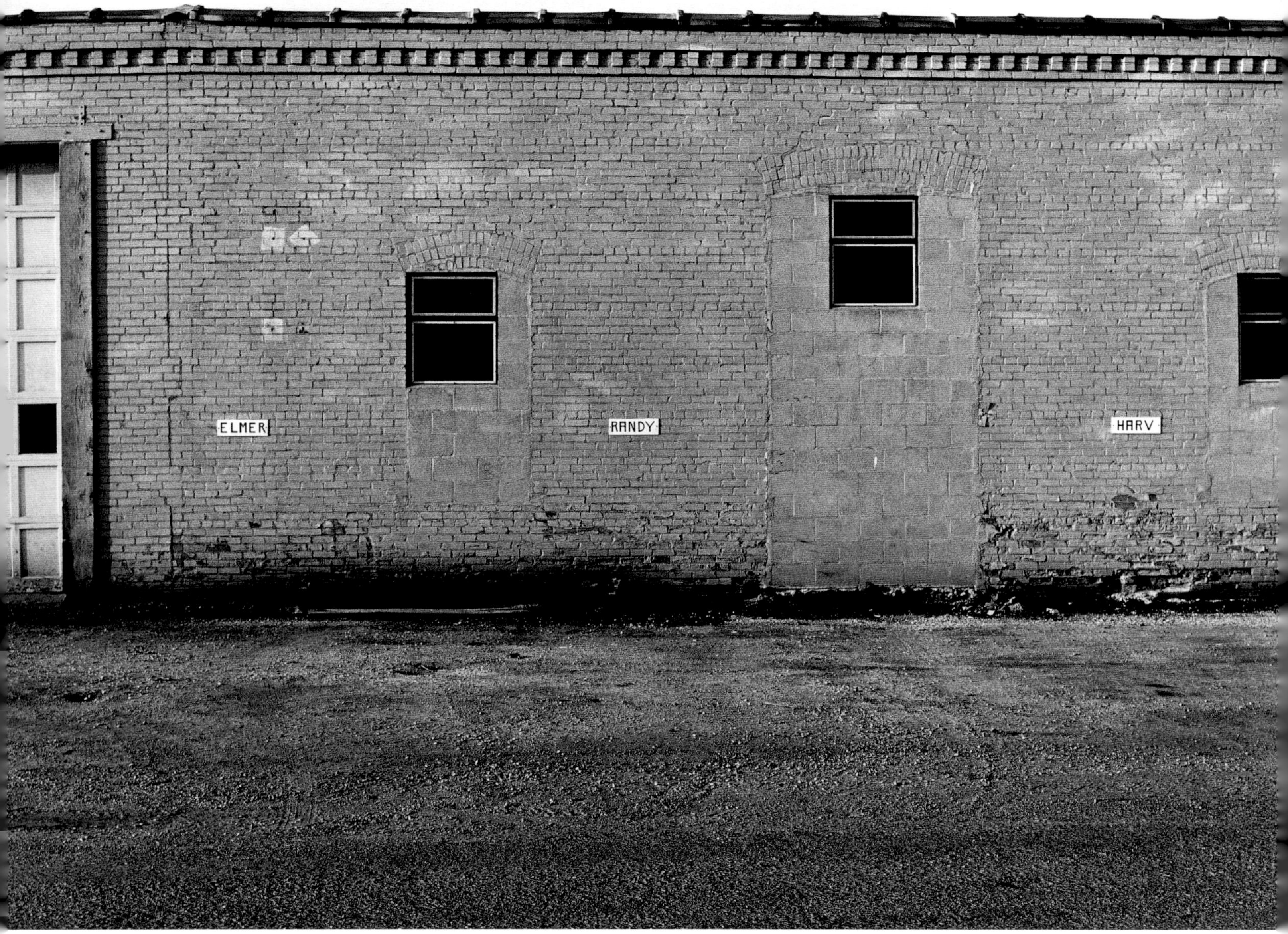
ELMER
RANDY
HARV

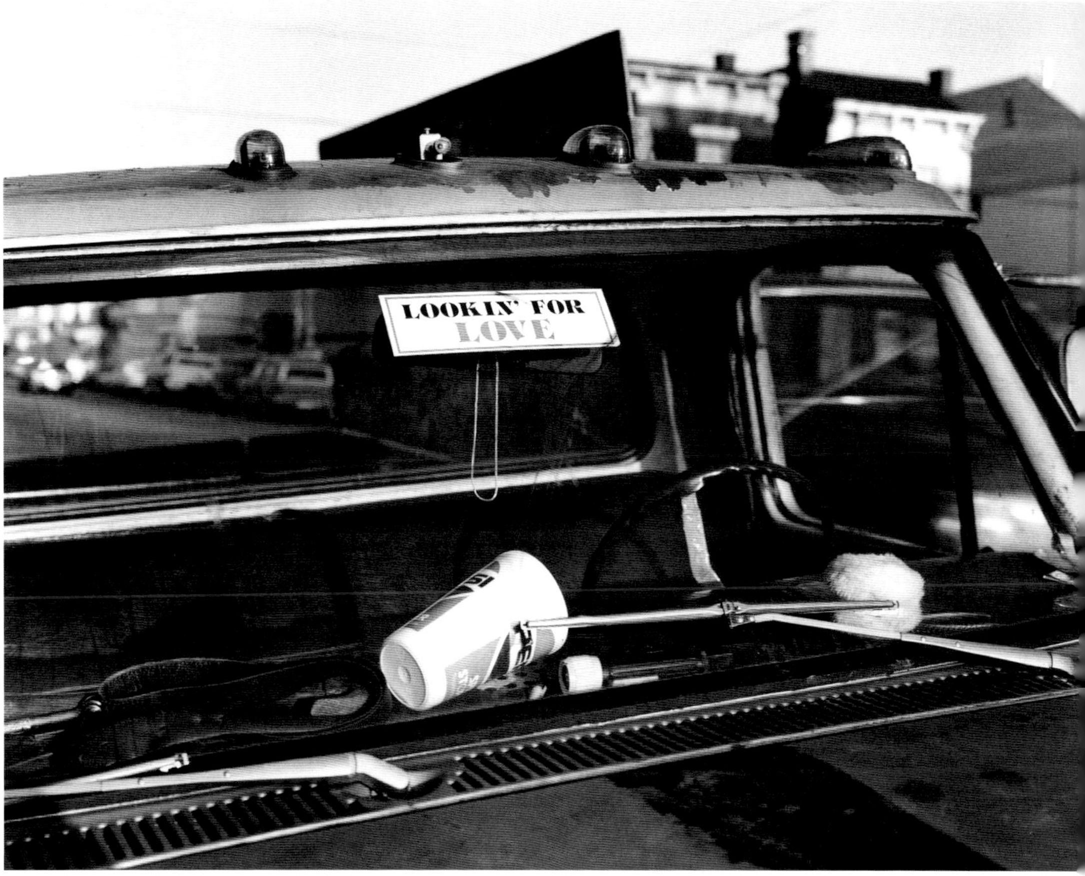
LOOKIN' FOR
LOVE

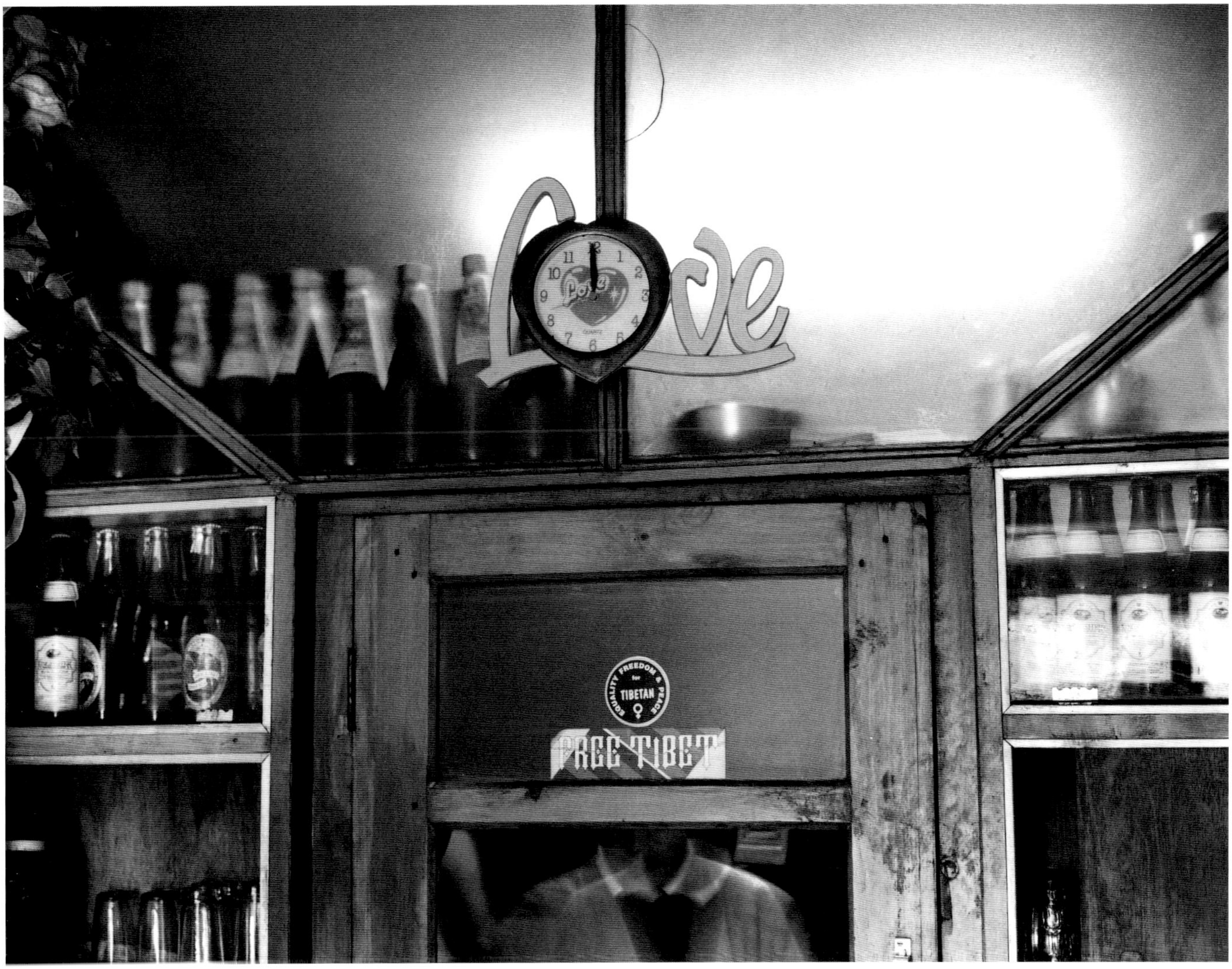
Love
EQUALITY FREEDOM & PEACE
for
TIBETAN
FREE TIBET

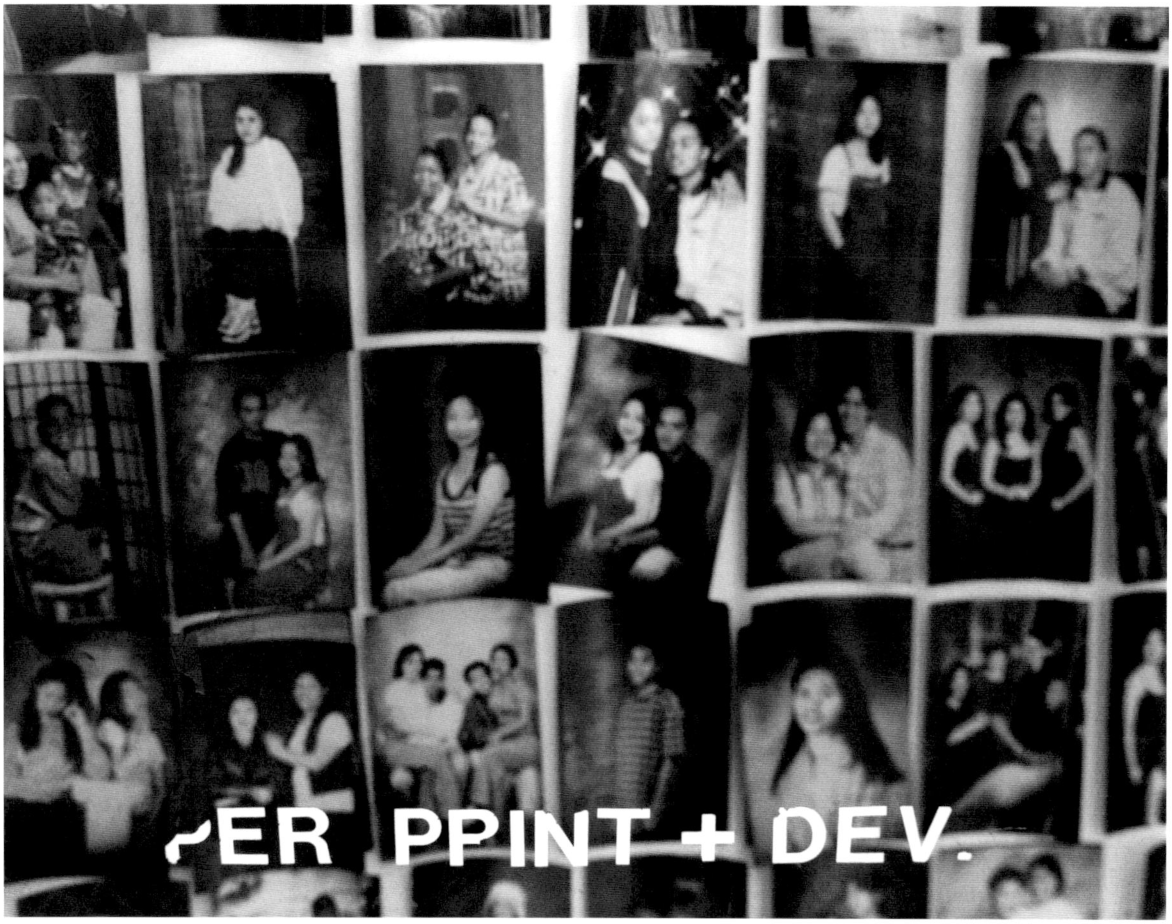
ER PPINT + DEV

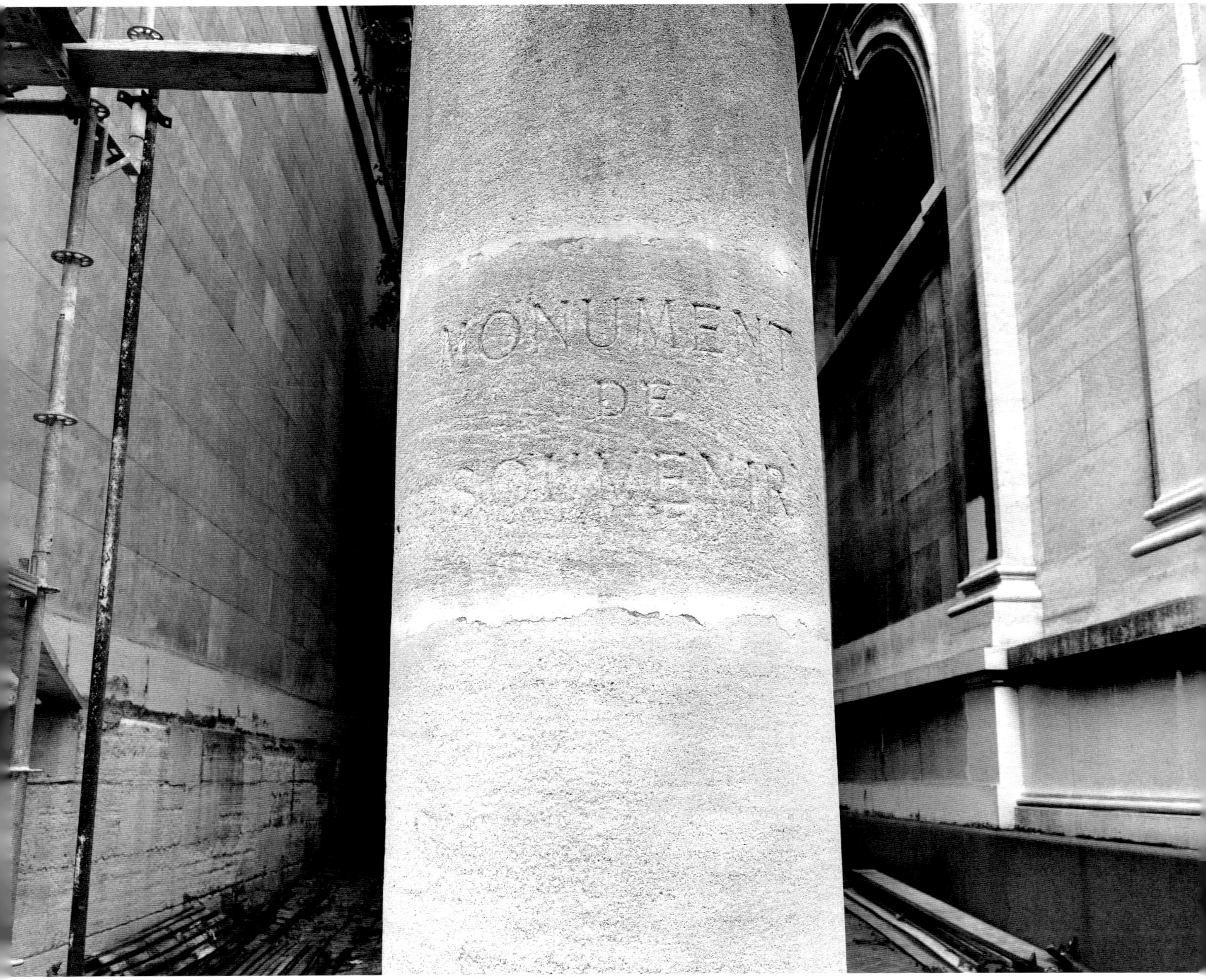
MONUMENT
DE

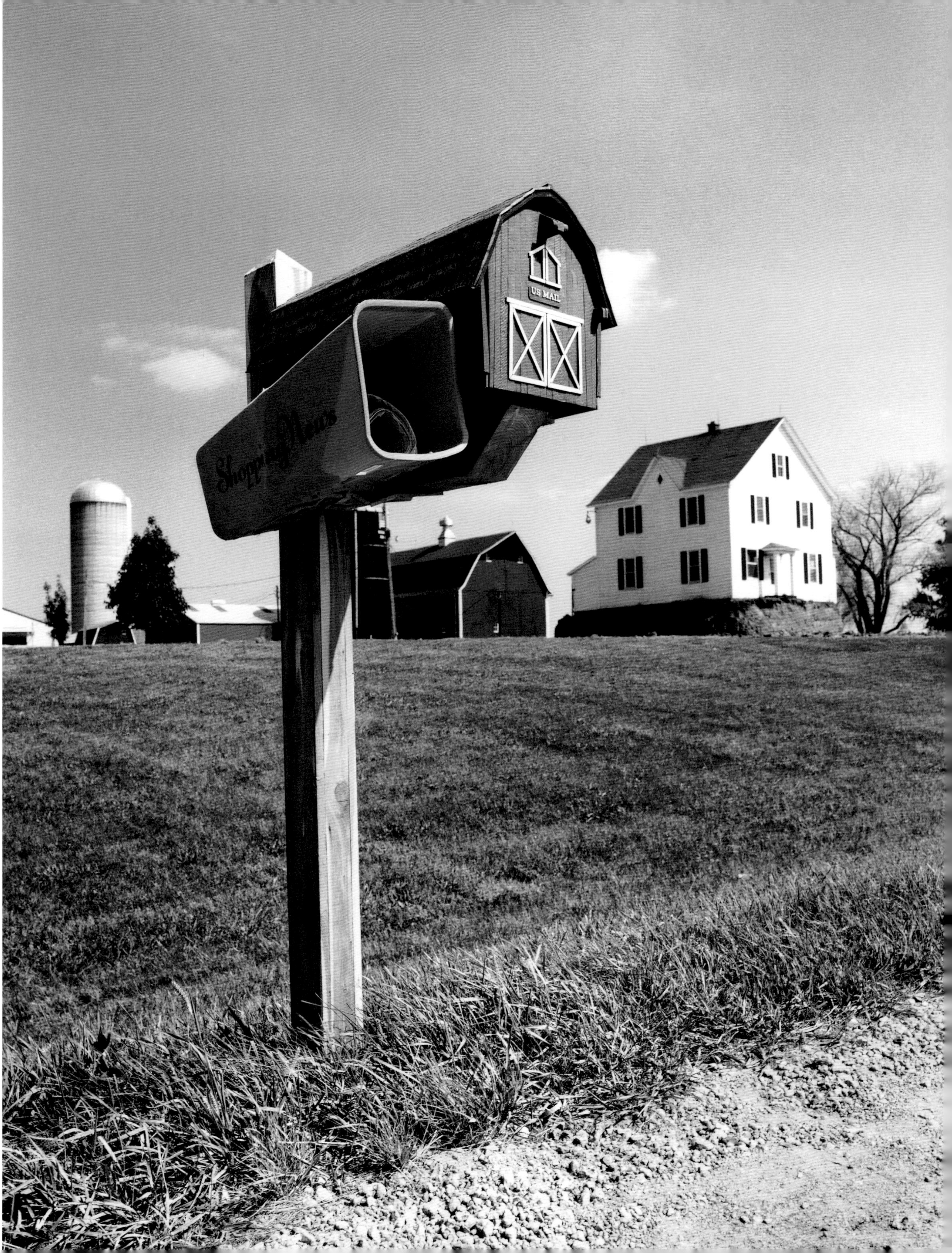
US MAIL
Shopping News

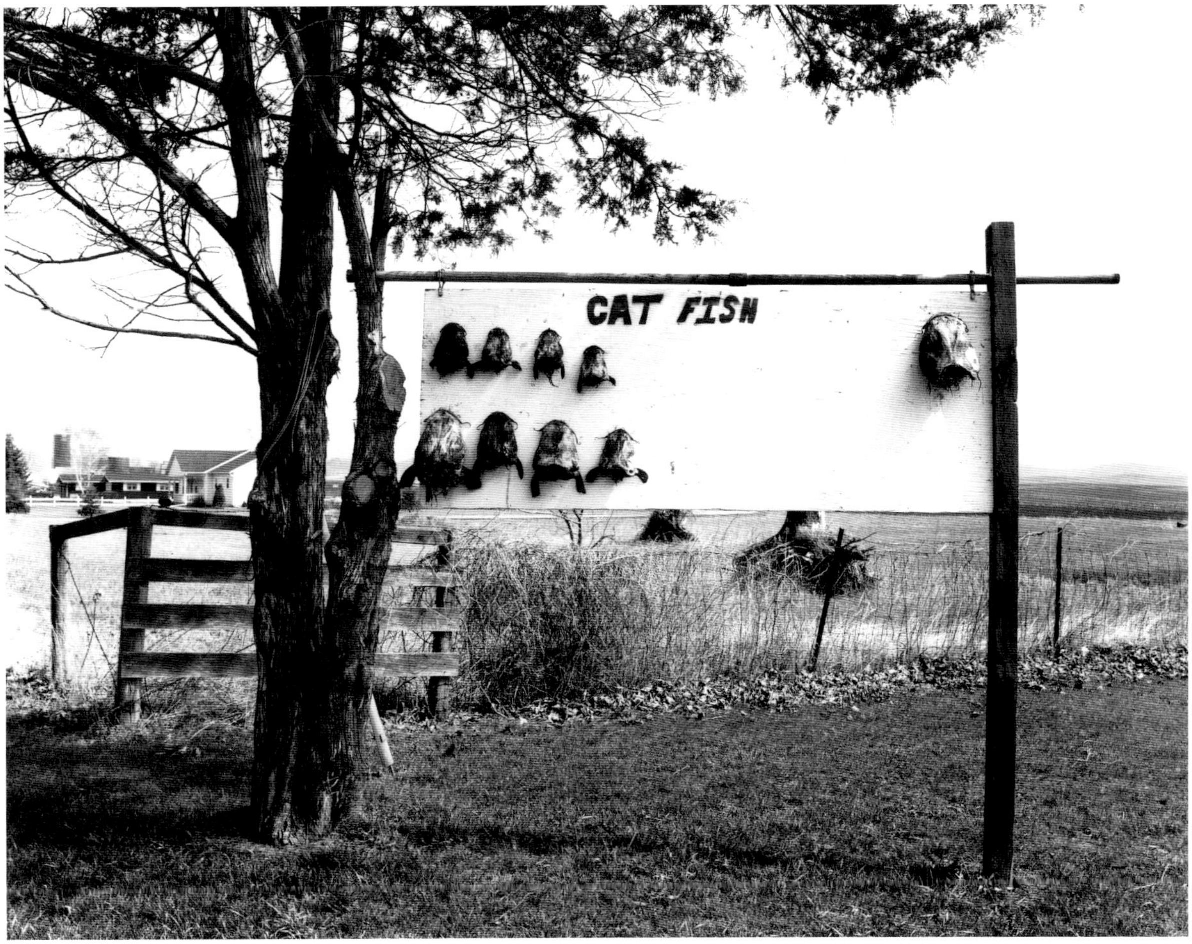
CAT FISH

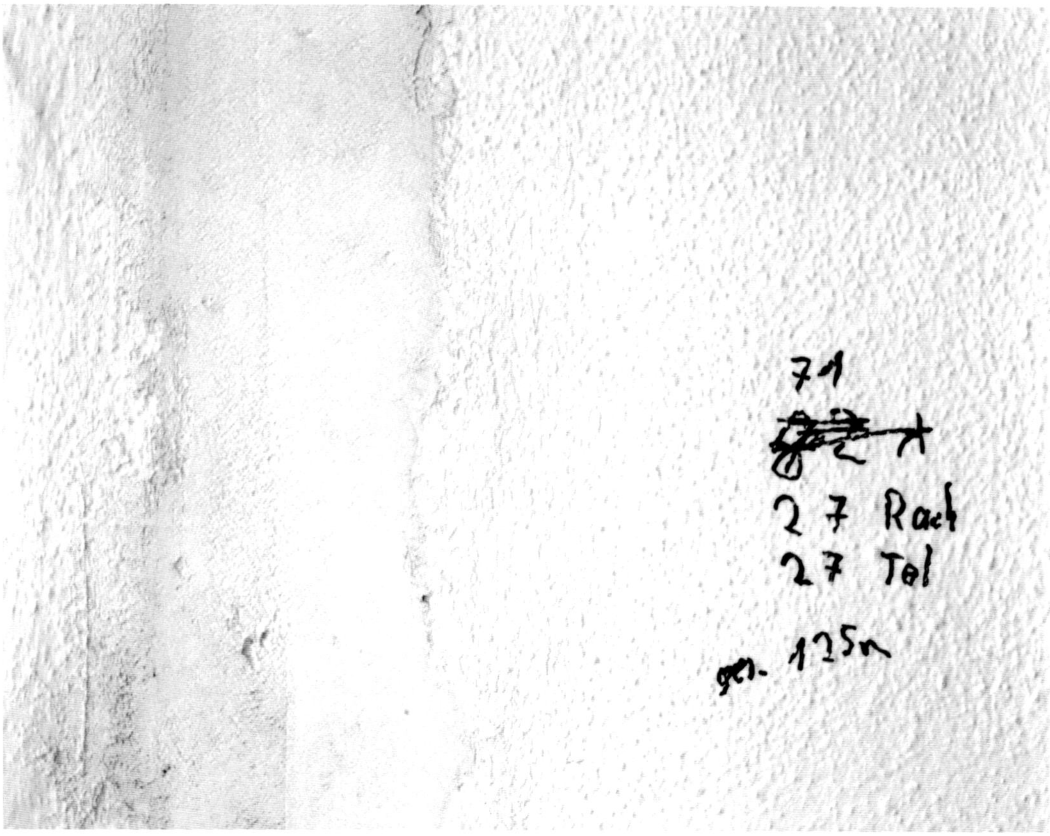
71
27 Rach
27 Tol
125m

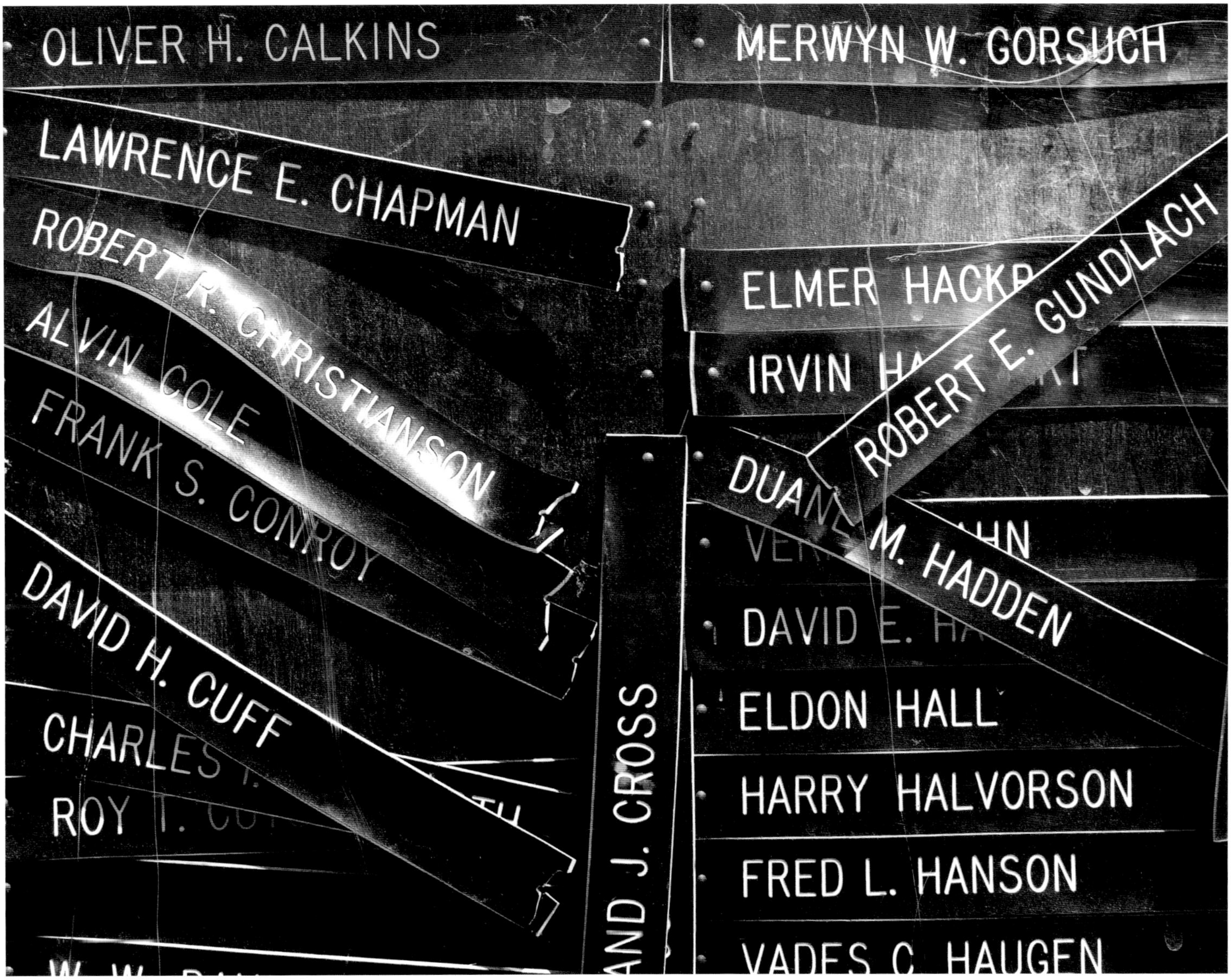
OLIVER H. CALKINS
MERWYN W. GORSUCH
LAWRENCE E. CHAPMAN
ROBERT R. CHRISTIANSON
ALVIN COLE
FRANK S. CONROY
DAVID H. CUFF
ELMER HACK
ROBERT E. GUNDLACH
IRVIN
DUANE M. HADDEN
DAVID E.
ELDON HALL
HARRY HALVORSON
FRED L. HANSON
VADES C. HAUGEN
AND J. CROSS
CHARLES
ROY

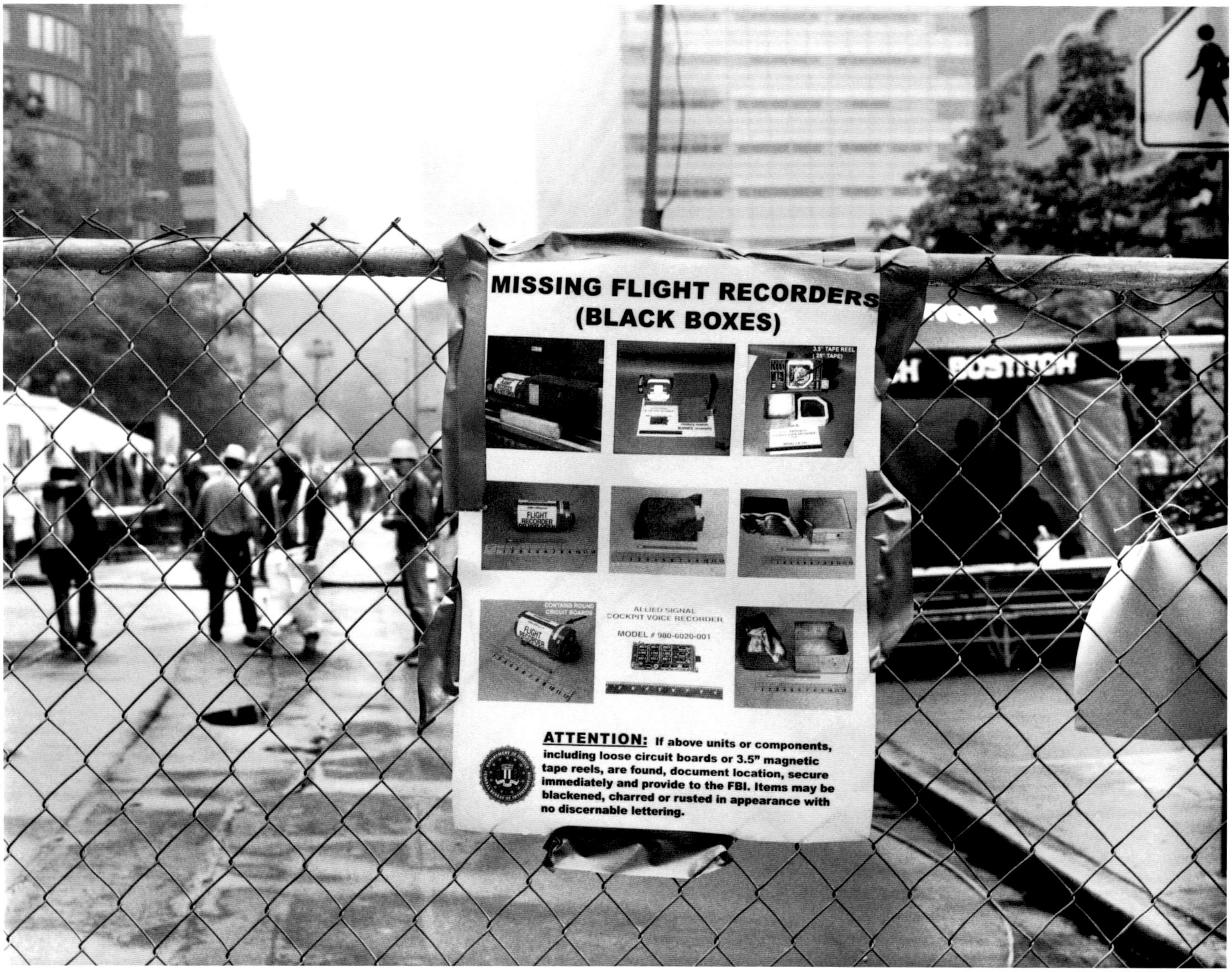
MISSING FLIGHT RECORDERS
(BLACK BOXES)
ALLIED SIGNAL
COCKPIT VOICE RECORDER
MODEL # 980-6020-001
ATTENTION: If above units or components, including loose circuit boards or 3.5" magnetic tape reels, are found, document location, secure immediately and provide to the FBI. Items may be blackened, charred or rusted in appearance with no discernable lettering.

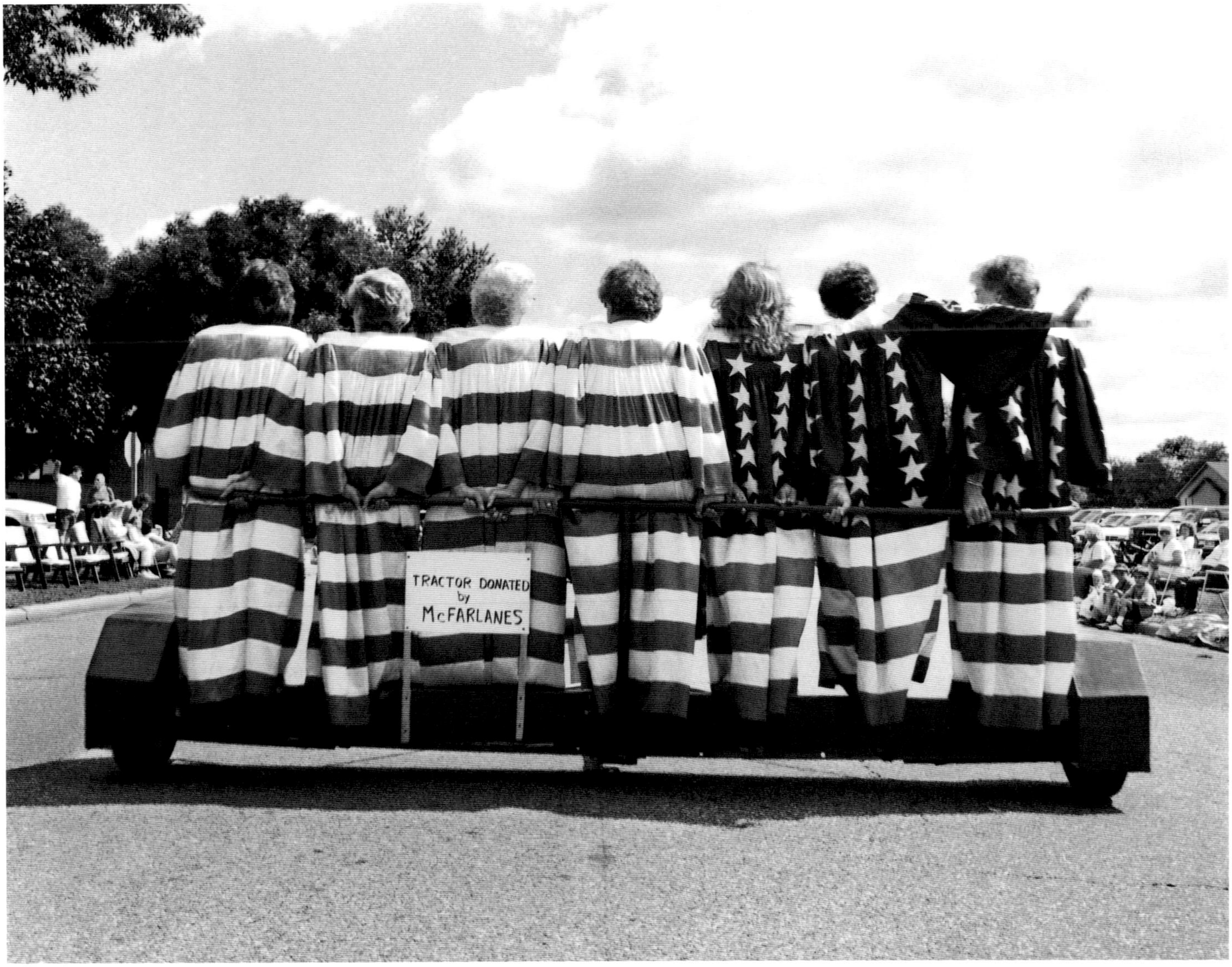
TRACTOR DONATED
by
McFARLANES

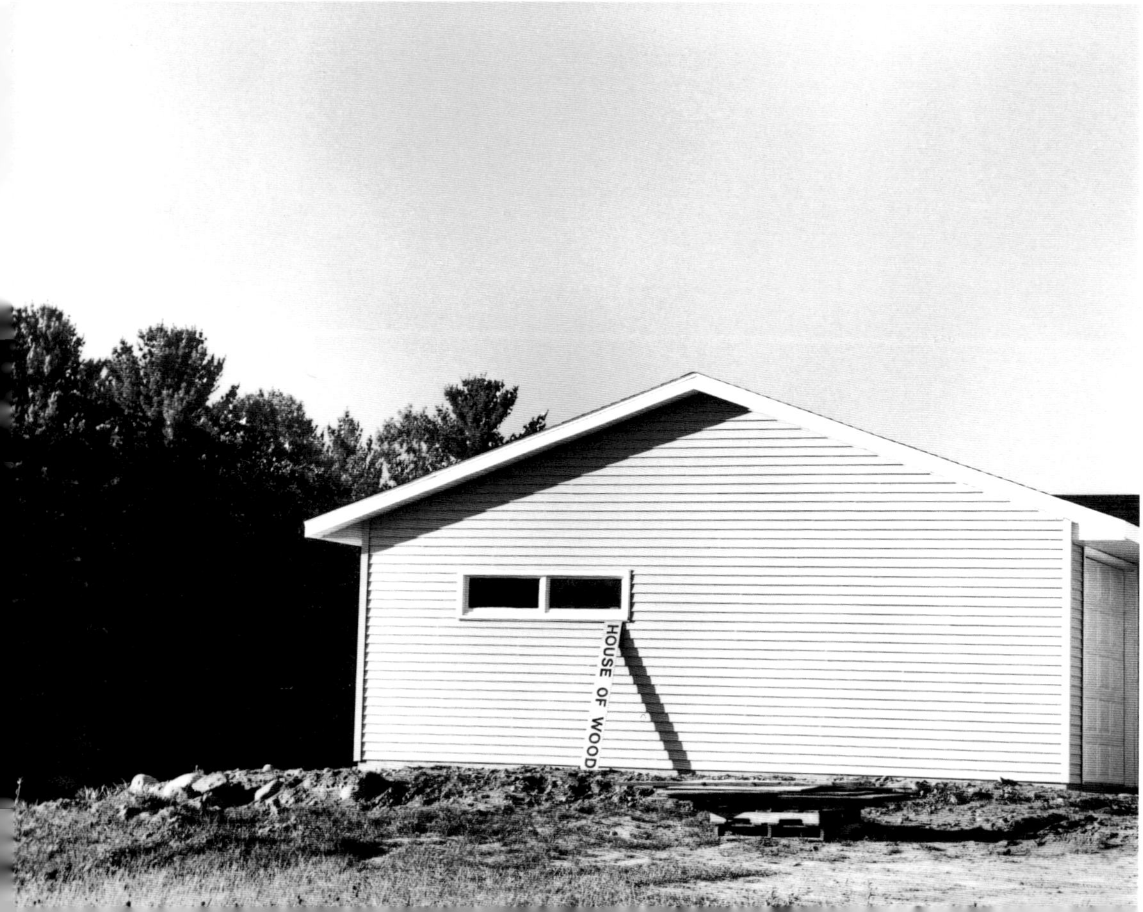
HOUSE OF WOOD

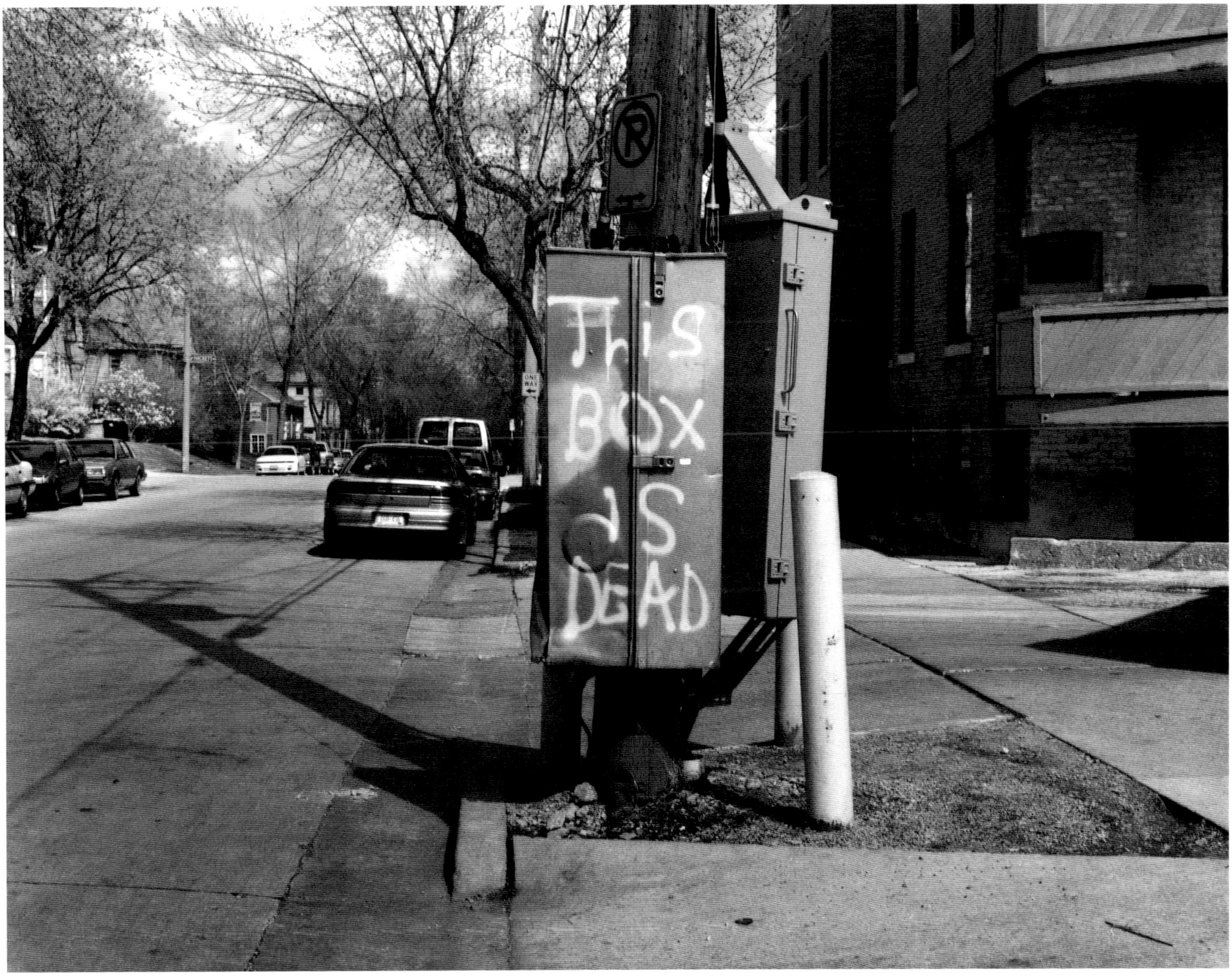
This BOX IS DEAD

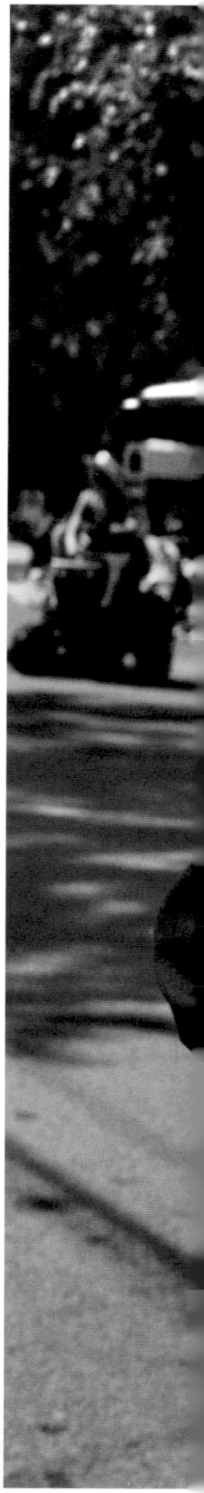

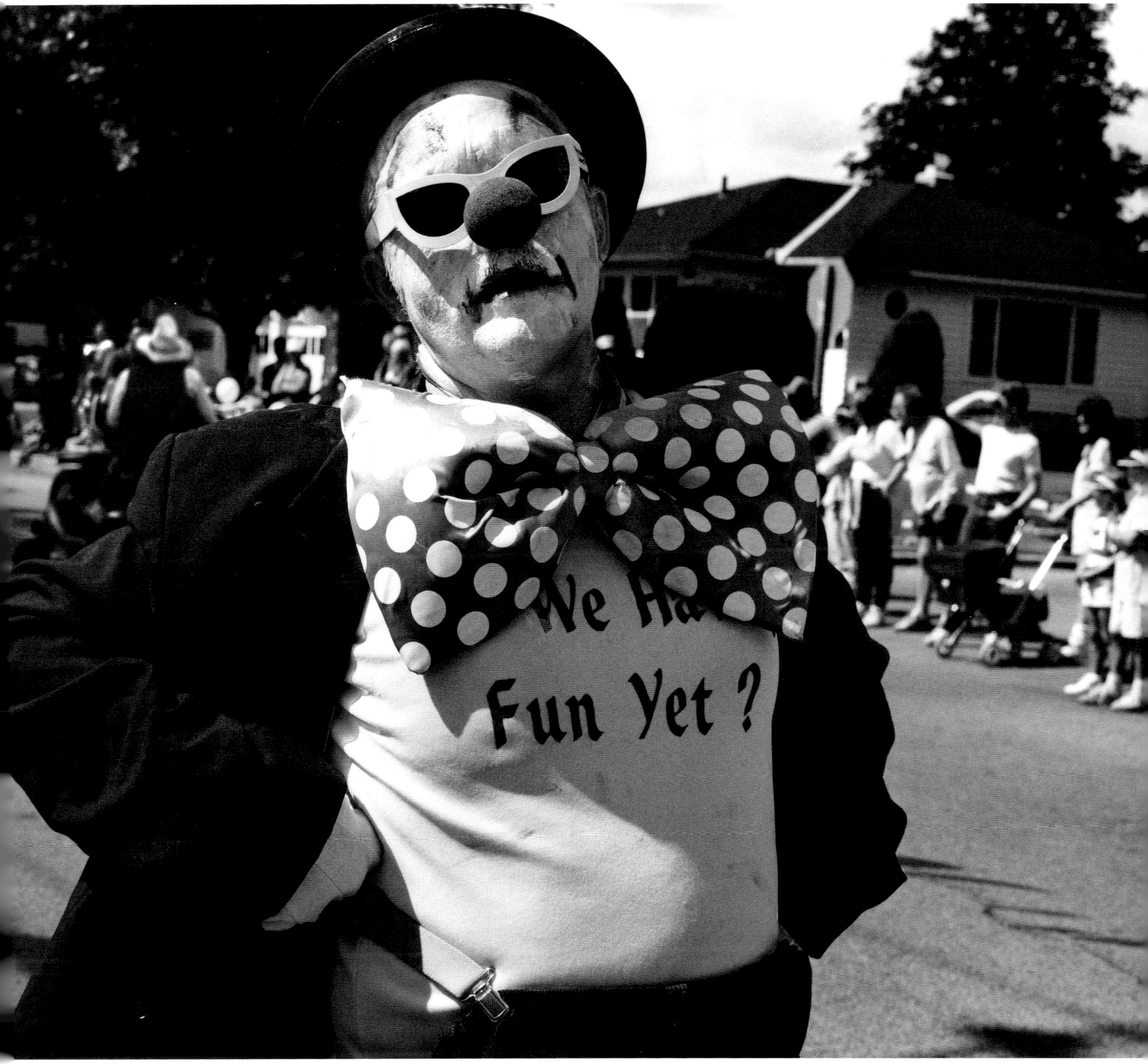
We Ha
Fun Yet ?

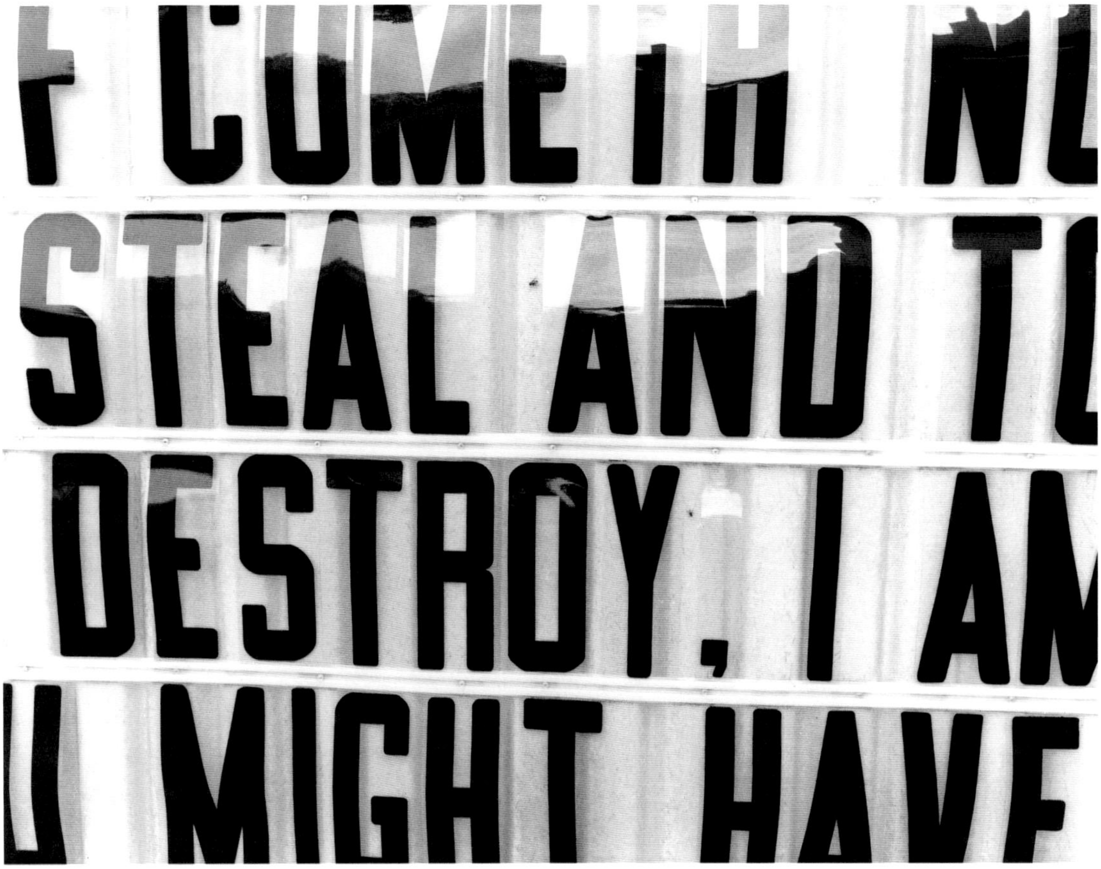
COMETH
STEAL AND
DESTROY, I
MIGHT

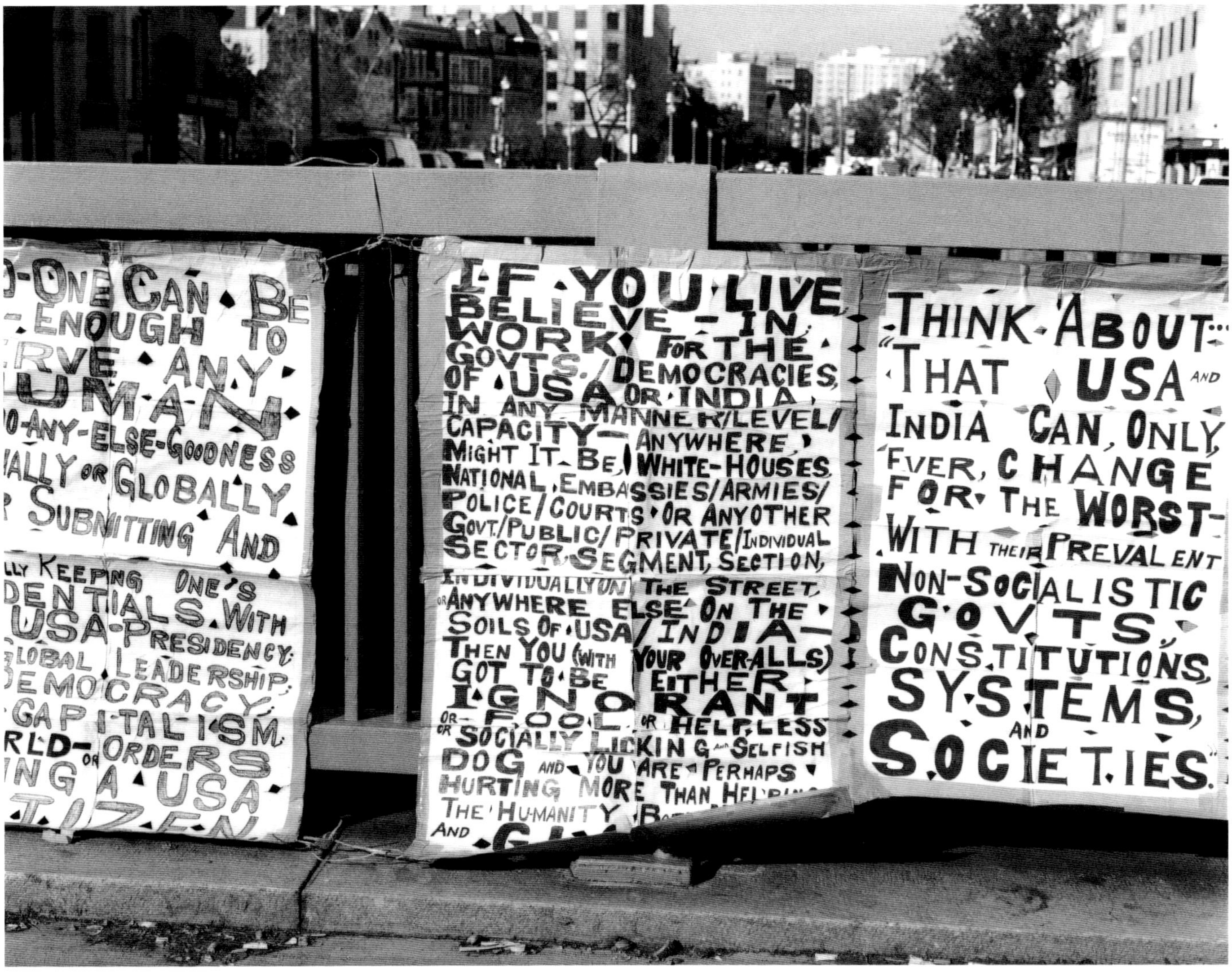
CAN BE
ENOUGH TO
ANY
OR GLOBALLY
SUBMITTING AND
KEEPING ONE'S
WITH
GLOBAL LEADERSHIP
CAPITALISM
ORDERS
A USA
IF YOU LIVE
BELIEVE – IN
WORK FOR THE
GOVTS./DEMOCRACIES
OF USA OR INDIA
IN ANY MANNER/LEVEL/
CAPACITY – ANYWHERE
MIGHT IT BE WHITE-HOUSES
NATIONAL EMBASSIES/ARMIES/
POLICE/COURTS OR ANYOTHER
GOVT/PUBLIC/PRIVATE/INDIVIDUAL
SECTOR SEGMENT SECTION
INDIVIDUALLY ON THE STREET
OR ANYWHERE ELSE ON THE
SOILS OF USA/INDIA –
THEN YOU (WITH YOUR OVER-ALLS)
GOT TO BE EITHER
IGNORANT
OR FOOL OR HELPLESS
OR SOCIALLY LICKING AND SELFISH
DOG AND YOU ARE PERHAPS
HURTING MORE THAN
THE HU-MANITY
AND
THINK ABOUT:
"THAT USA AND
INDIA CAN ONLY
EVER CHANGE
FOR THE WORST –
WITH THEIR PREVALENT
NON-SOCIALISTIC
GOVTS,
CONSTITUTIONS,
SYSTEMS,
AND
SOCIETIES."

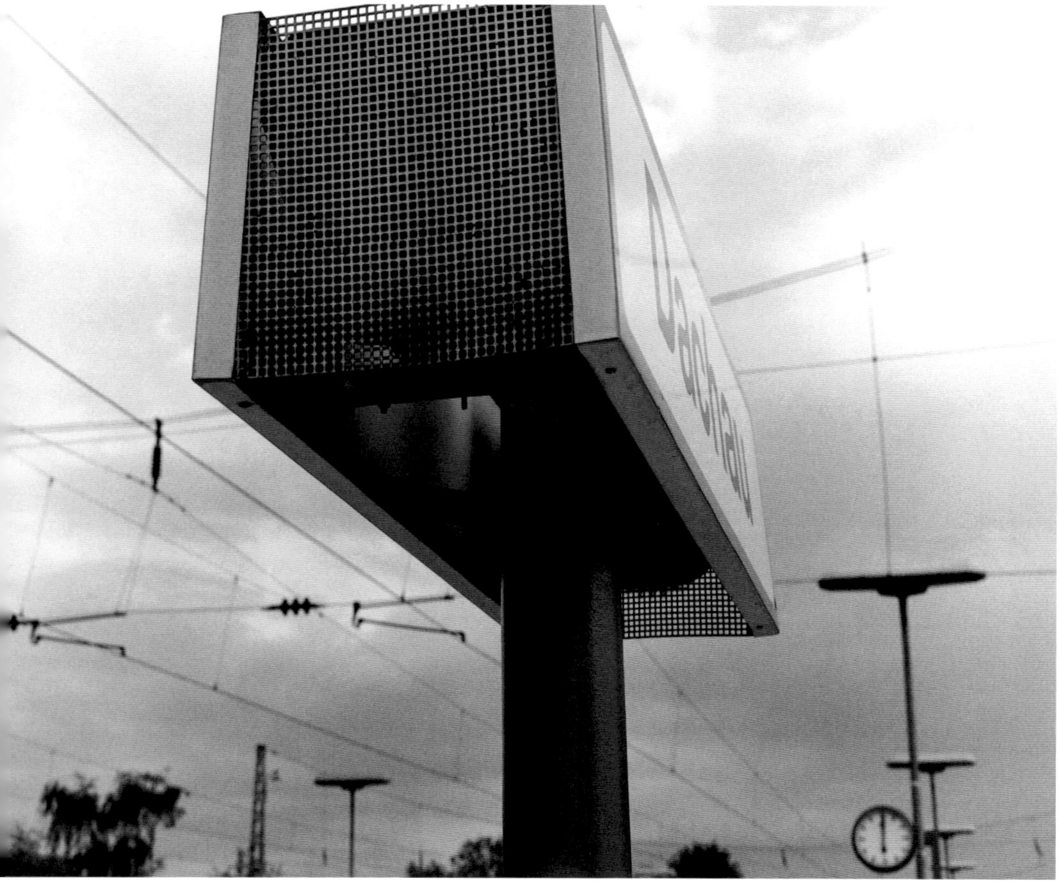
Dachau

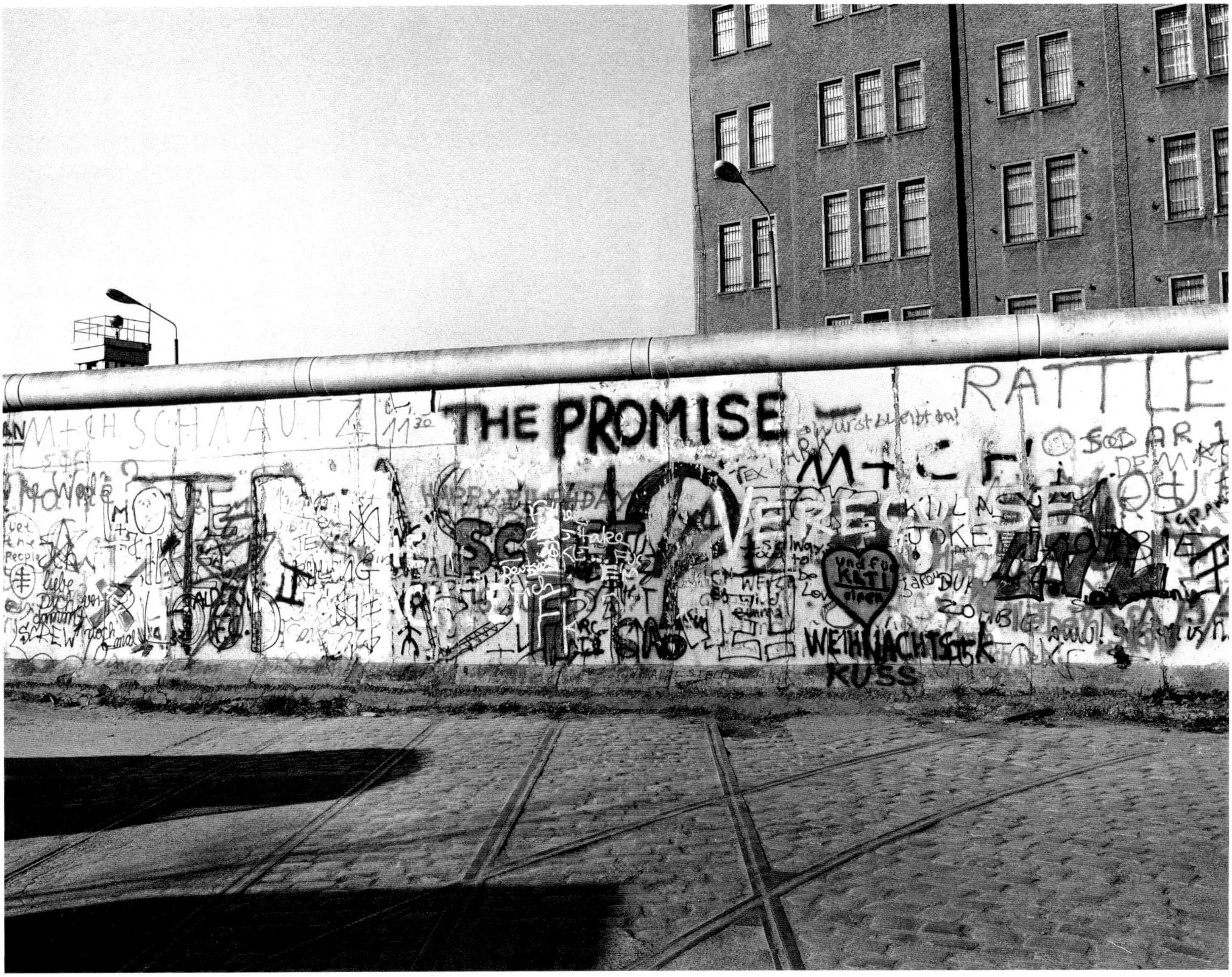
THE PROMISE
RATTLE
WEIHNACHTS
KUSS

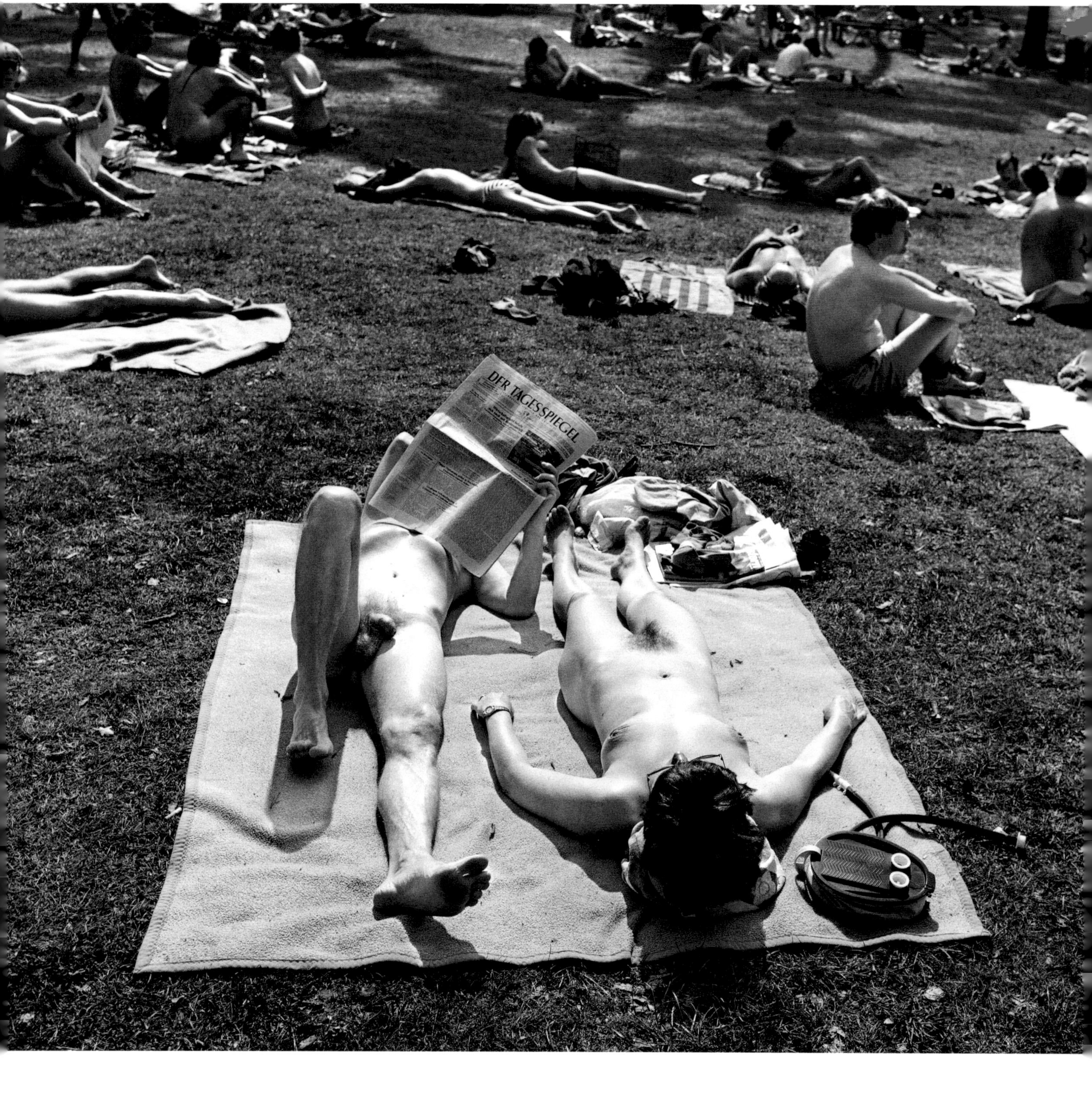
DER TAGESSPIEGEL

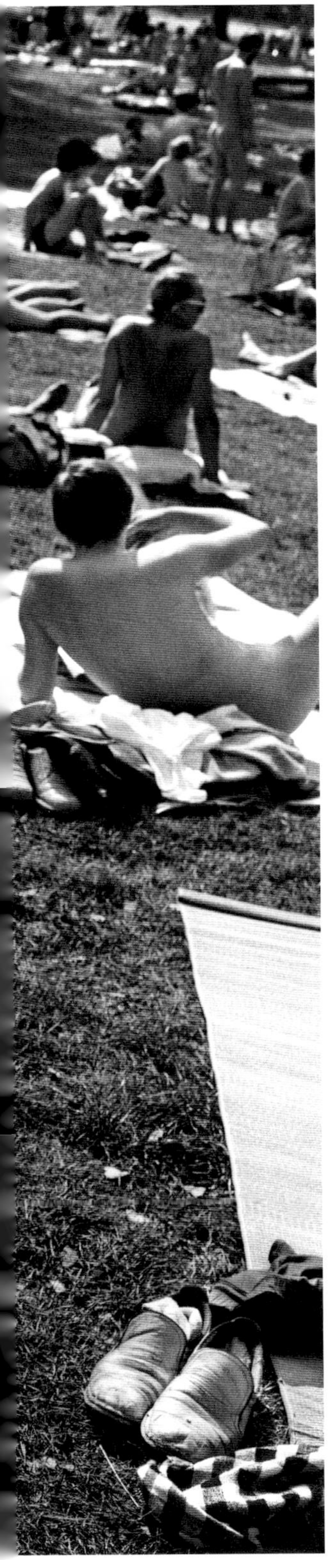

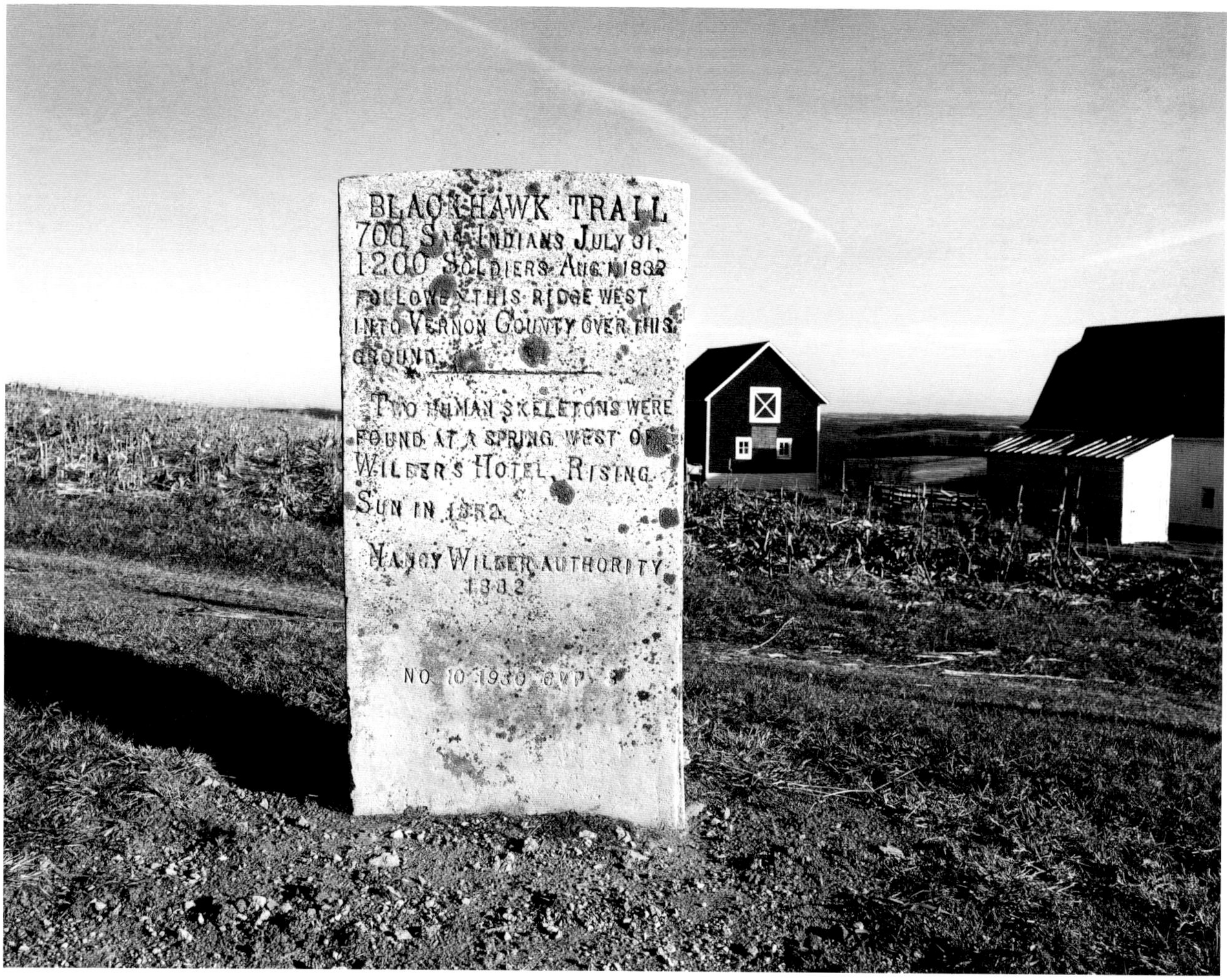
HAWK TRAIL
INDIANS JULY 31
1200 SOLDIERS
THIS RIDGE WEST
VERNON COUNTY OVER THIS
GROUND
SKELETONS WERE
FOUND AT A SPRING WEST
HOTEL, RISING
SUN IN
AUTHORITY
NO 10 1930

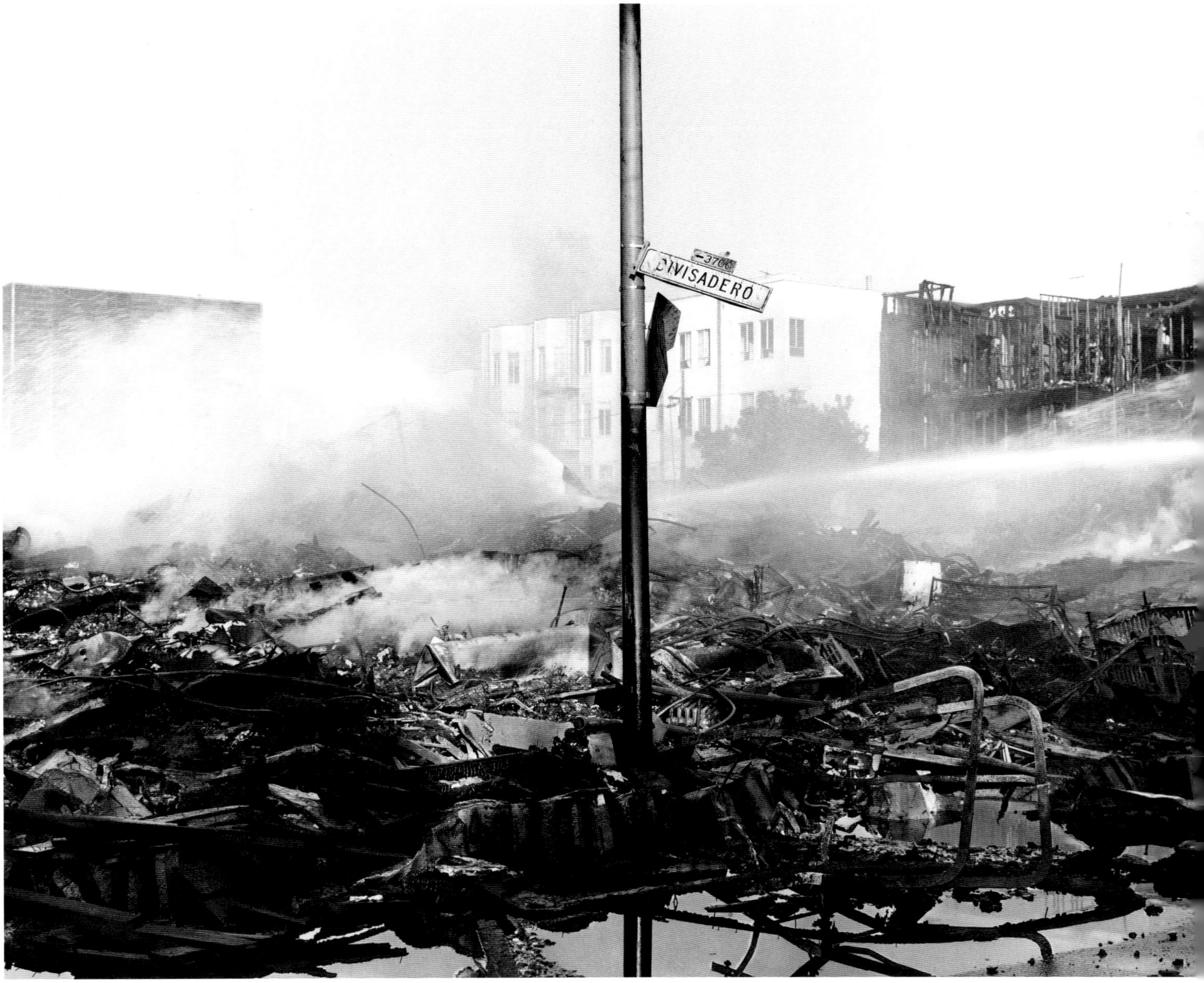
3700
DIVISADERO

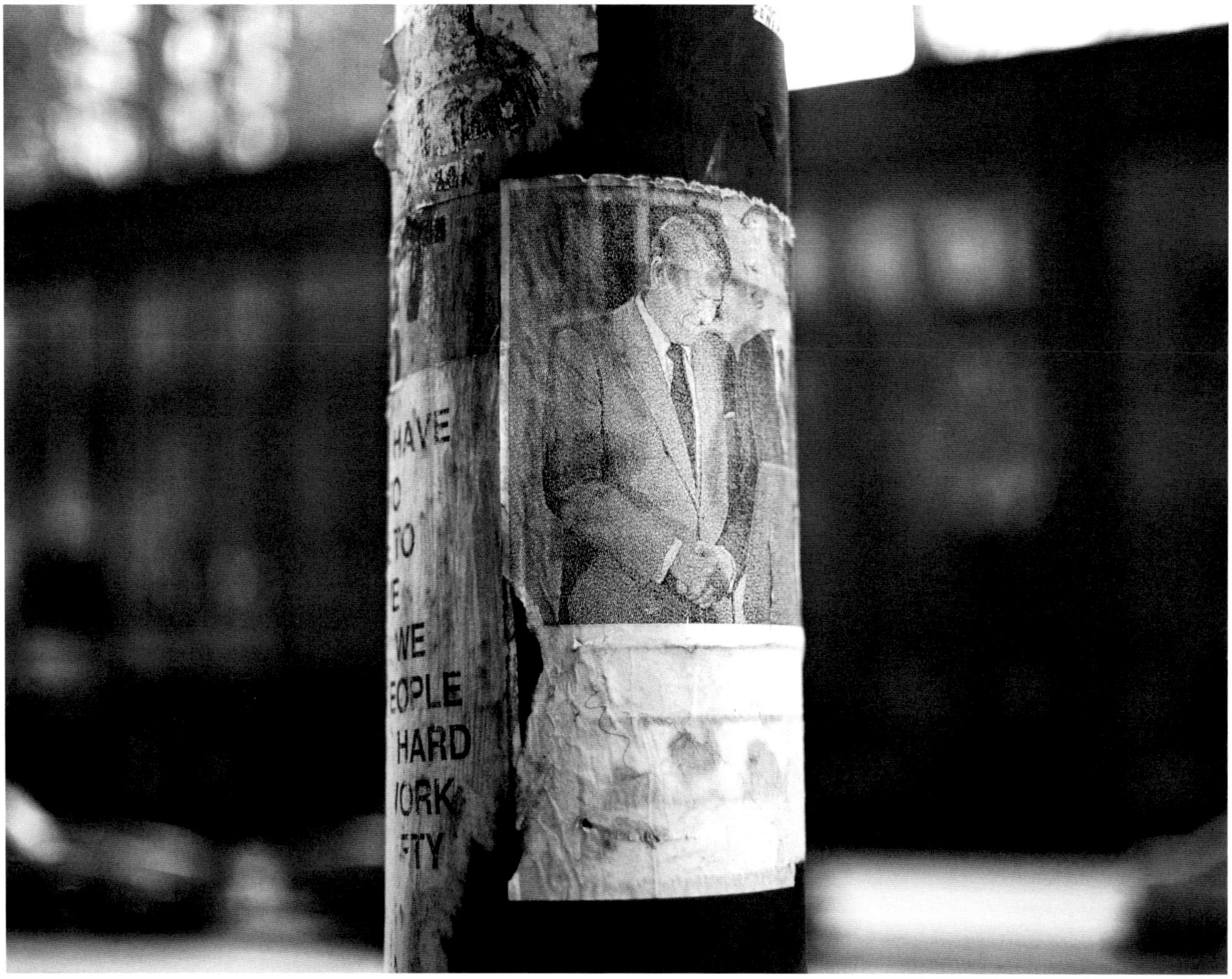
HAVE
TO
WE
EOPLE
HARD

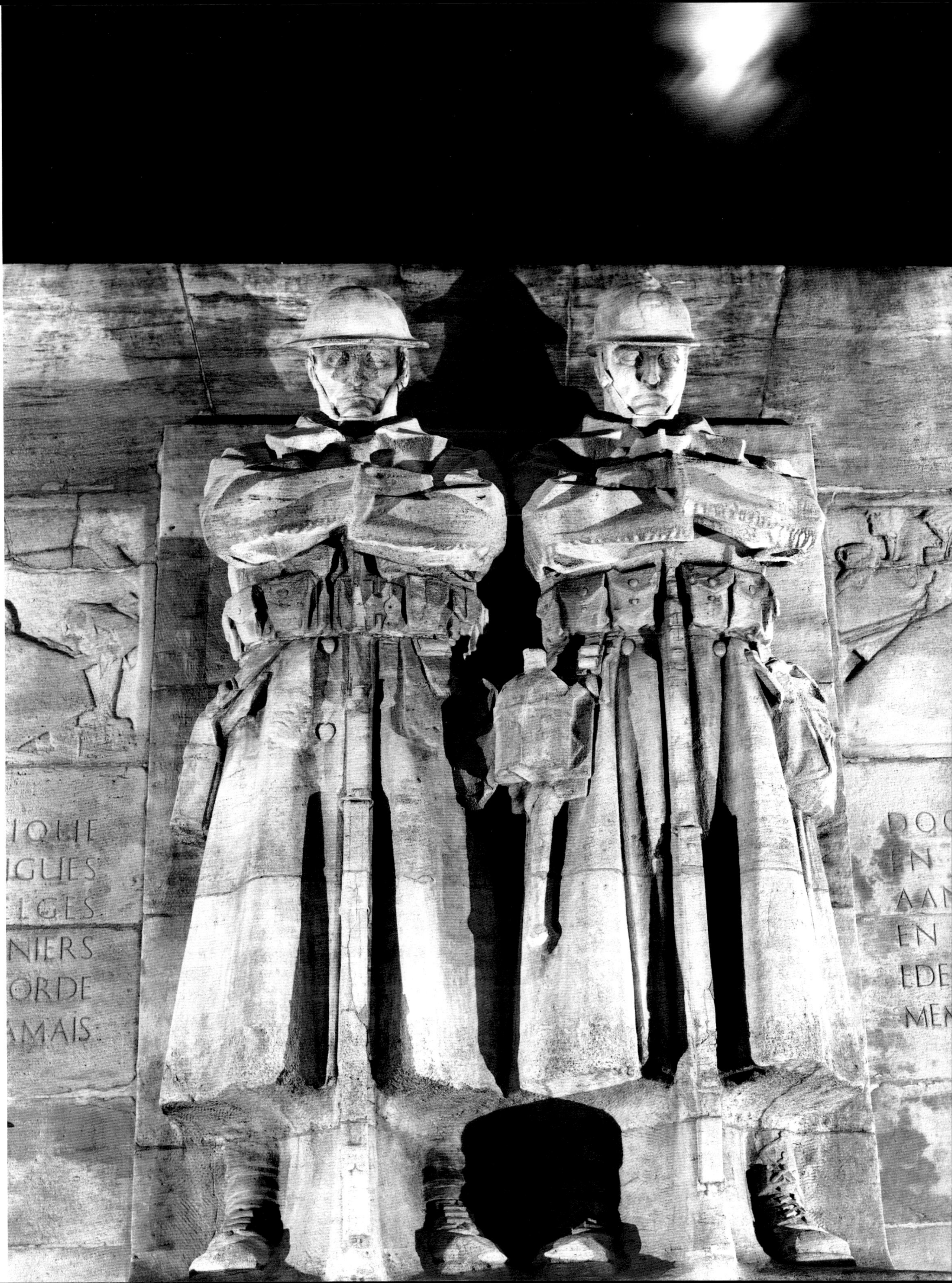

IQUE
IGUES
ELGES
NIERS
ORDE
AMAIS
DOC
EN
AAN
EN
EDE
MEN

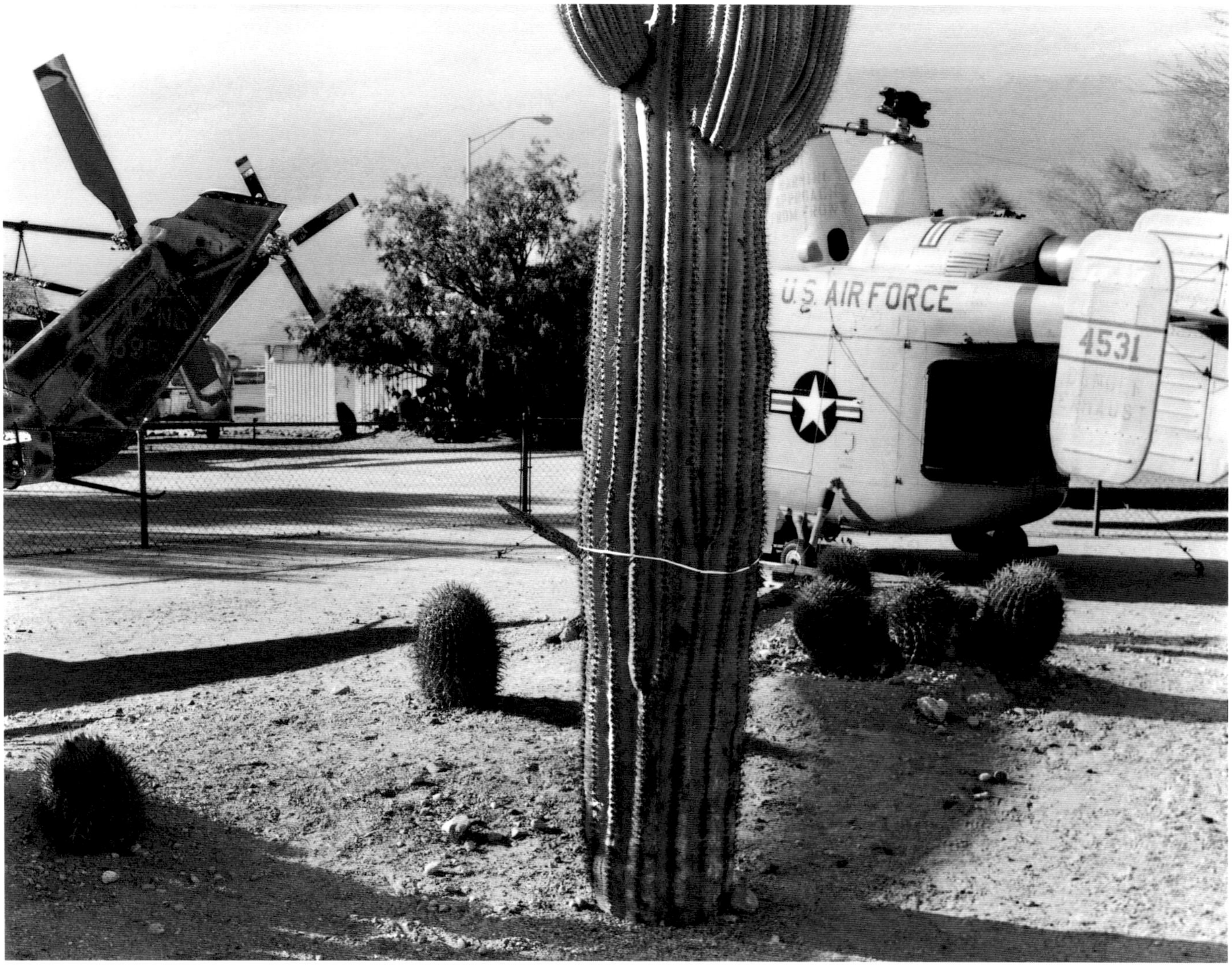
U.S. AIR FORCE
4531

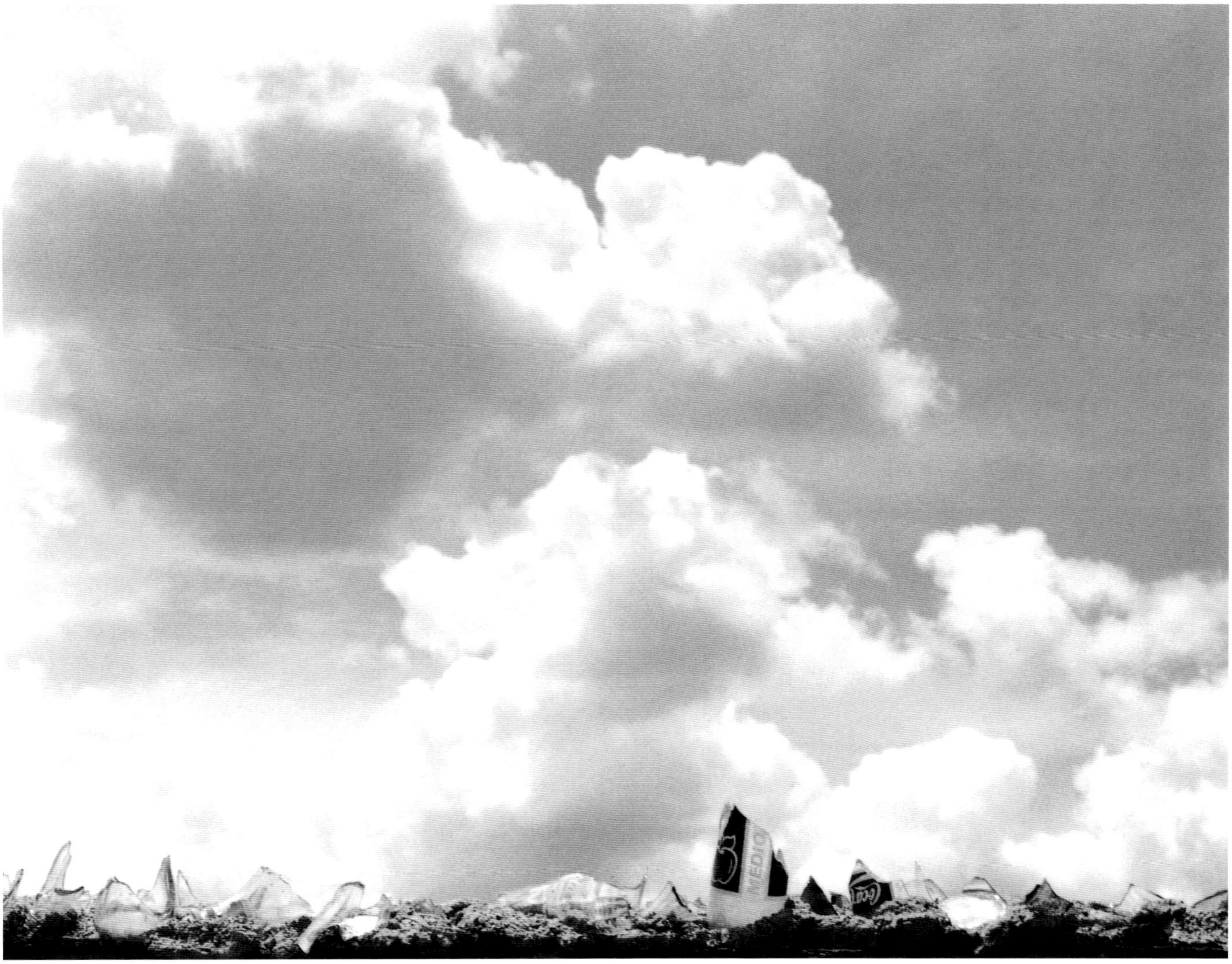

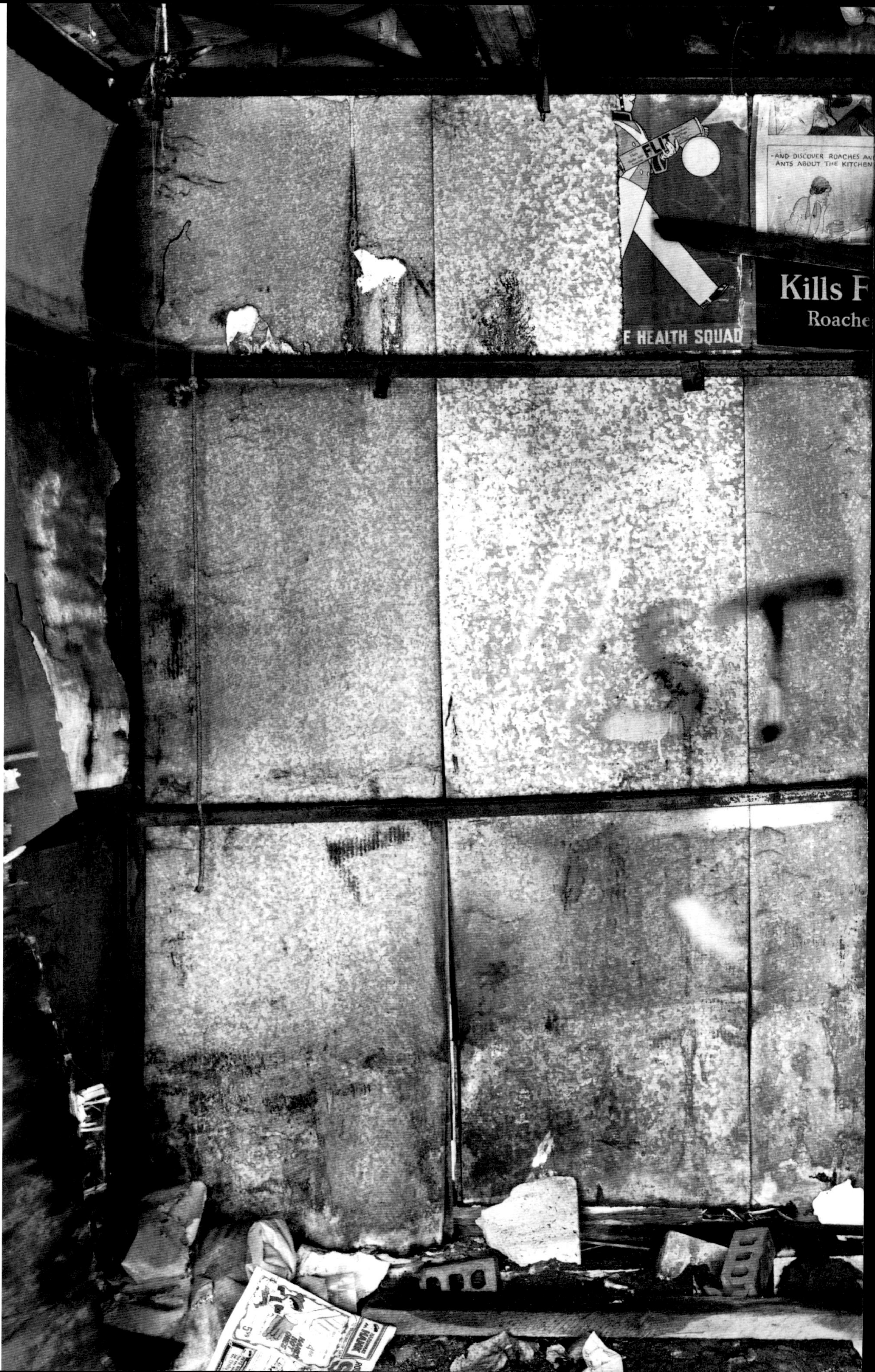
FLIT
-AND DISCOVER ROACHES AN
ANTS ABOUT THE KITCHEN
E HEALTH SQUAD
Kills F
Roache

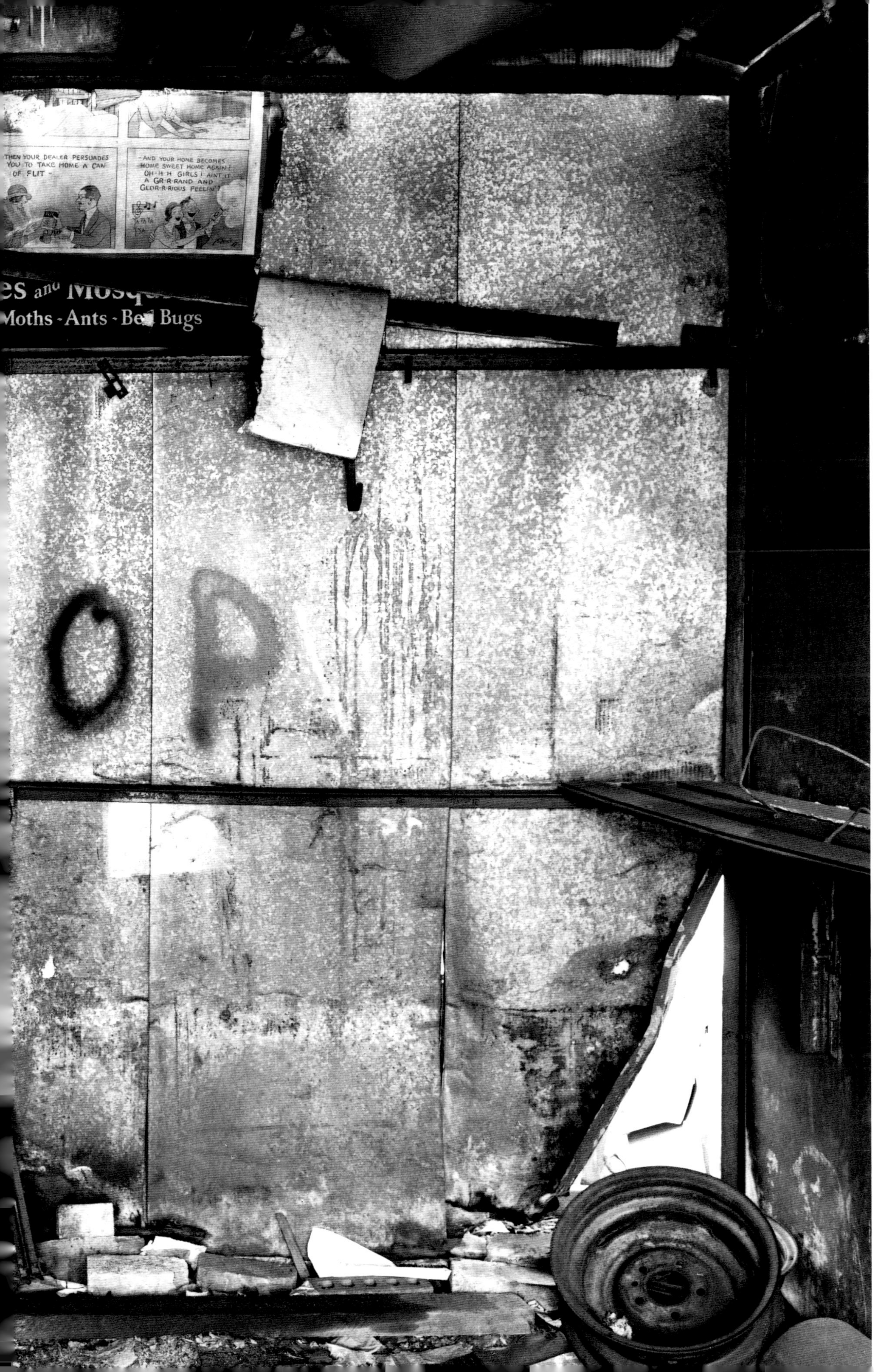

THEN YOUR DEALER PERSUADES YOU TO TAKE HOME A CAN OF FLIT -
- AND YOUR HOME BECOMES HOME SWEET HOME AGAIN! OH-H H GIRLS! AINT IT A GR-R-RAND AND GLOR-R-RIOUS FEELIN'?
es and Mosq
Moths - Ants - Be Bugs
OP

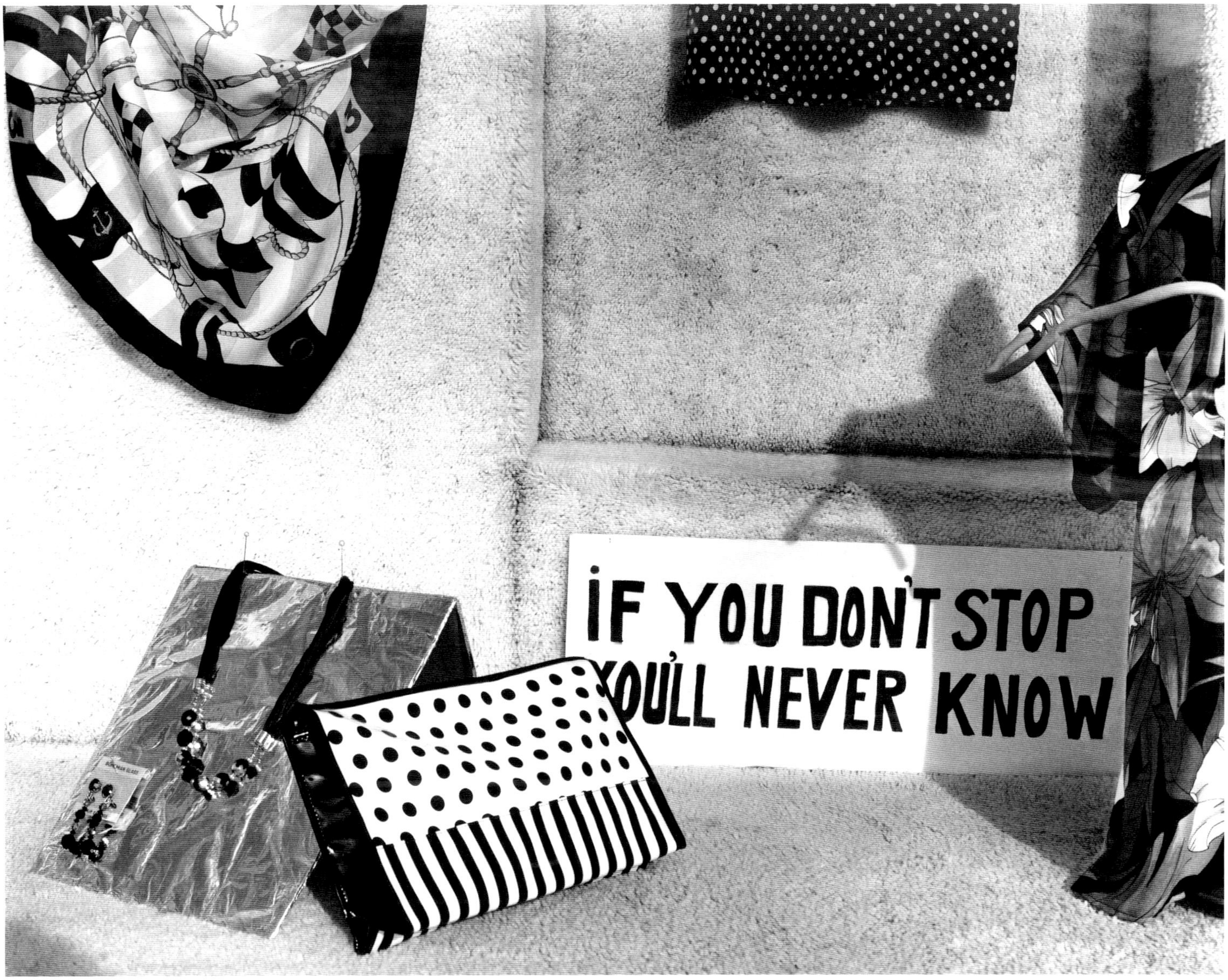
IF YOU DON'T STOP
YOU'LL NEVER KNOW

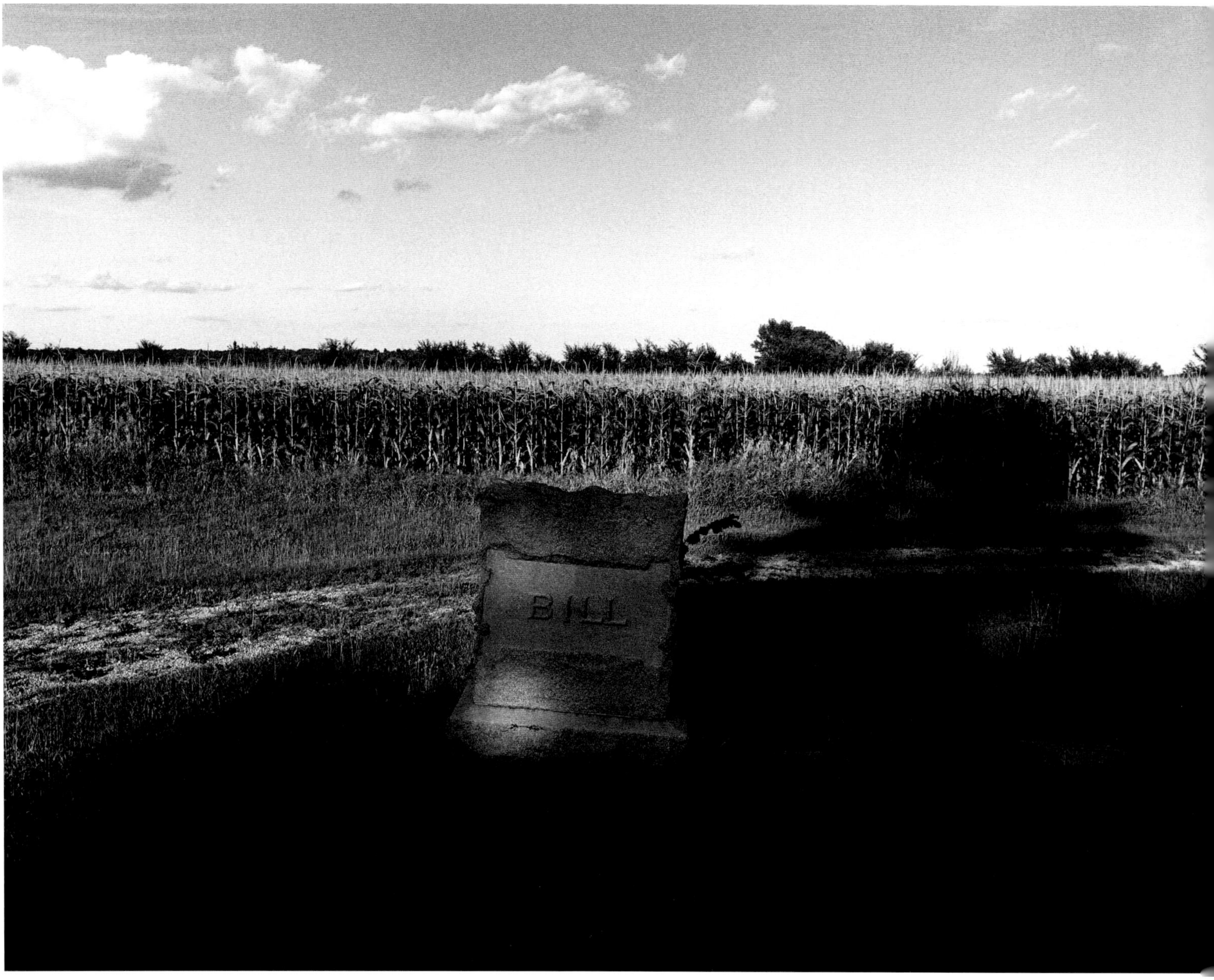
BILL

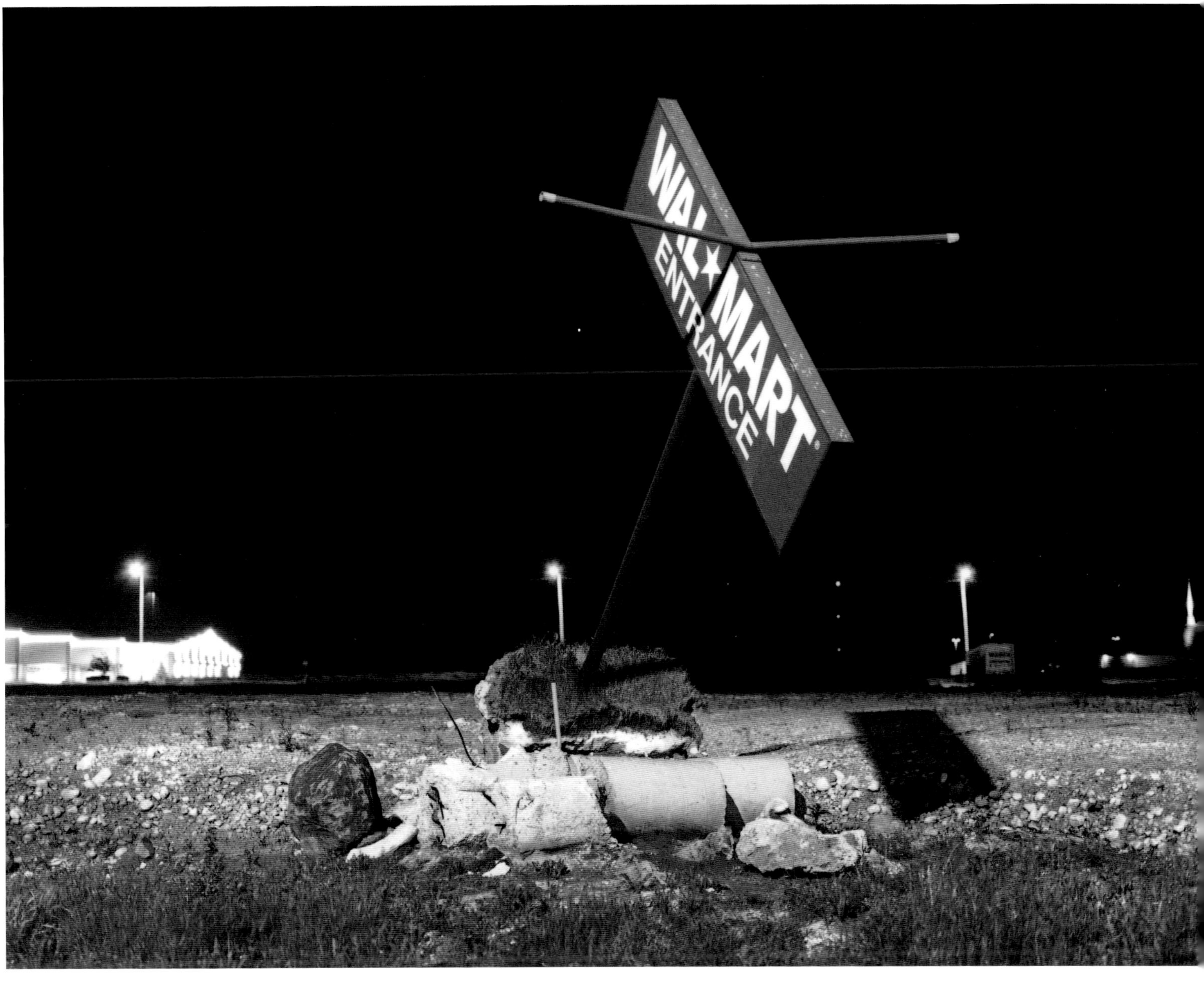
WAL★MART
ENTRANCE

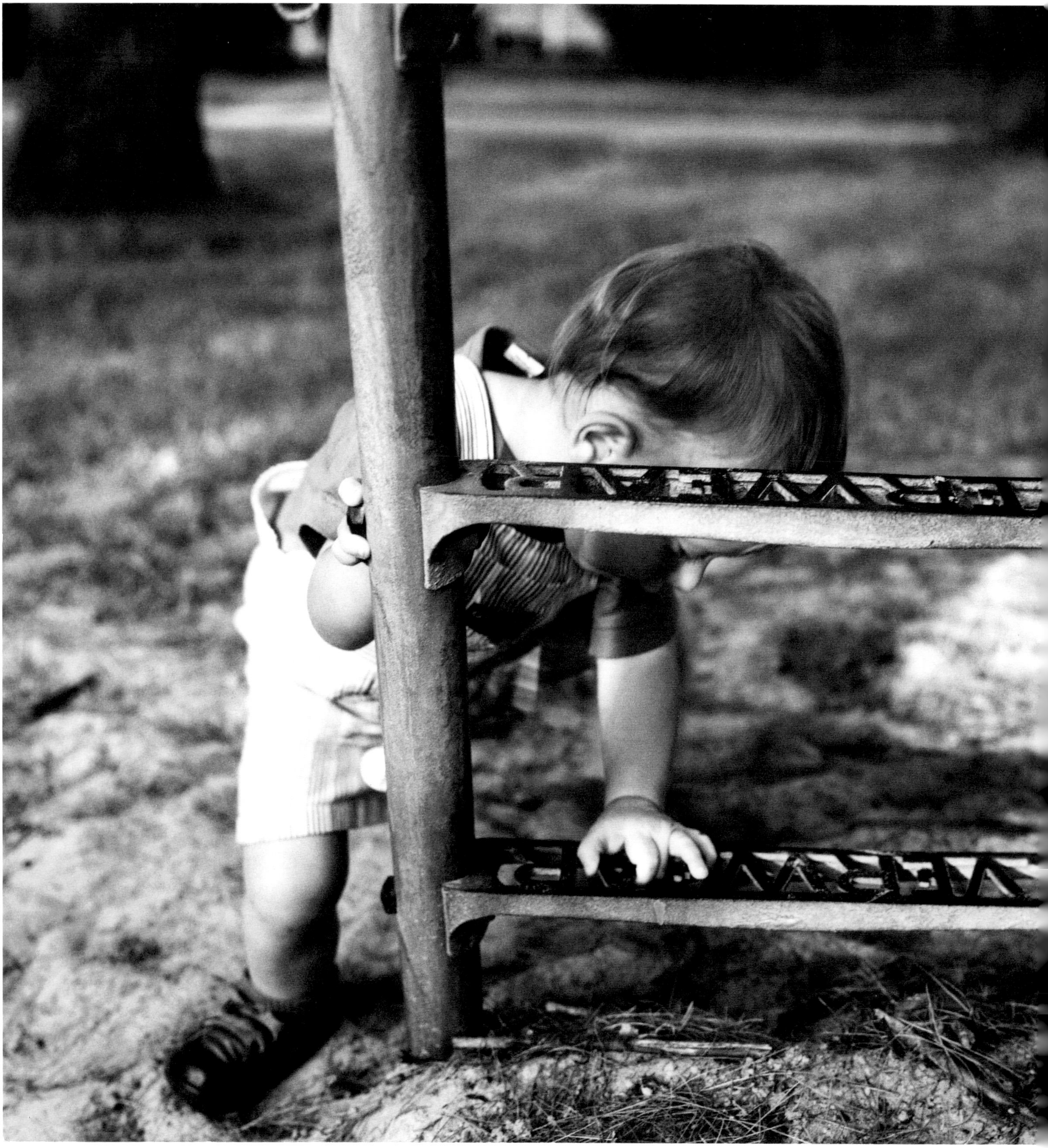

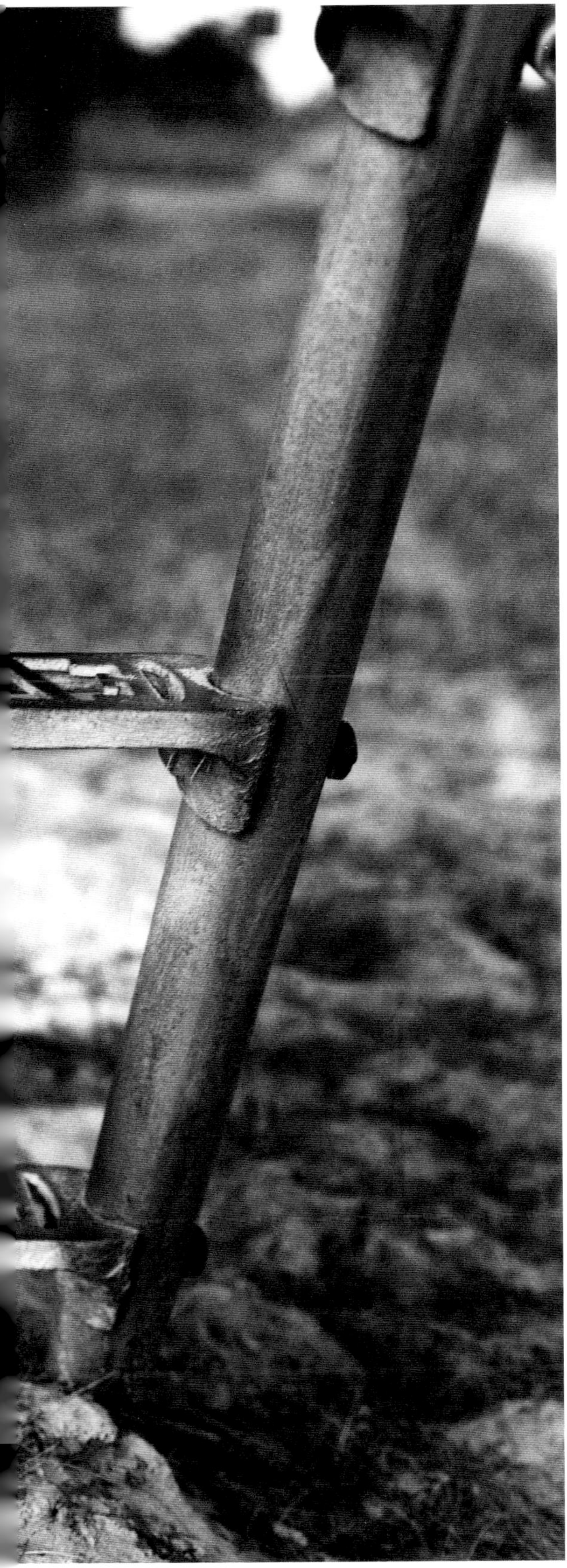

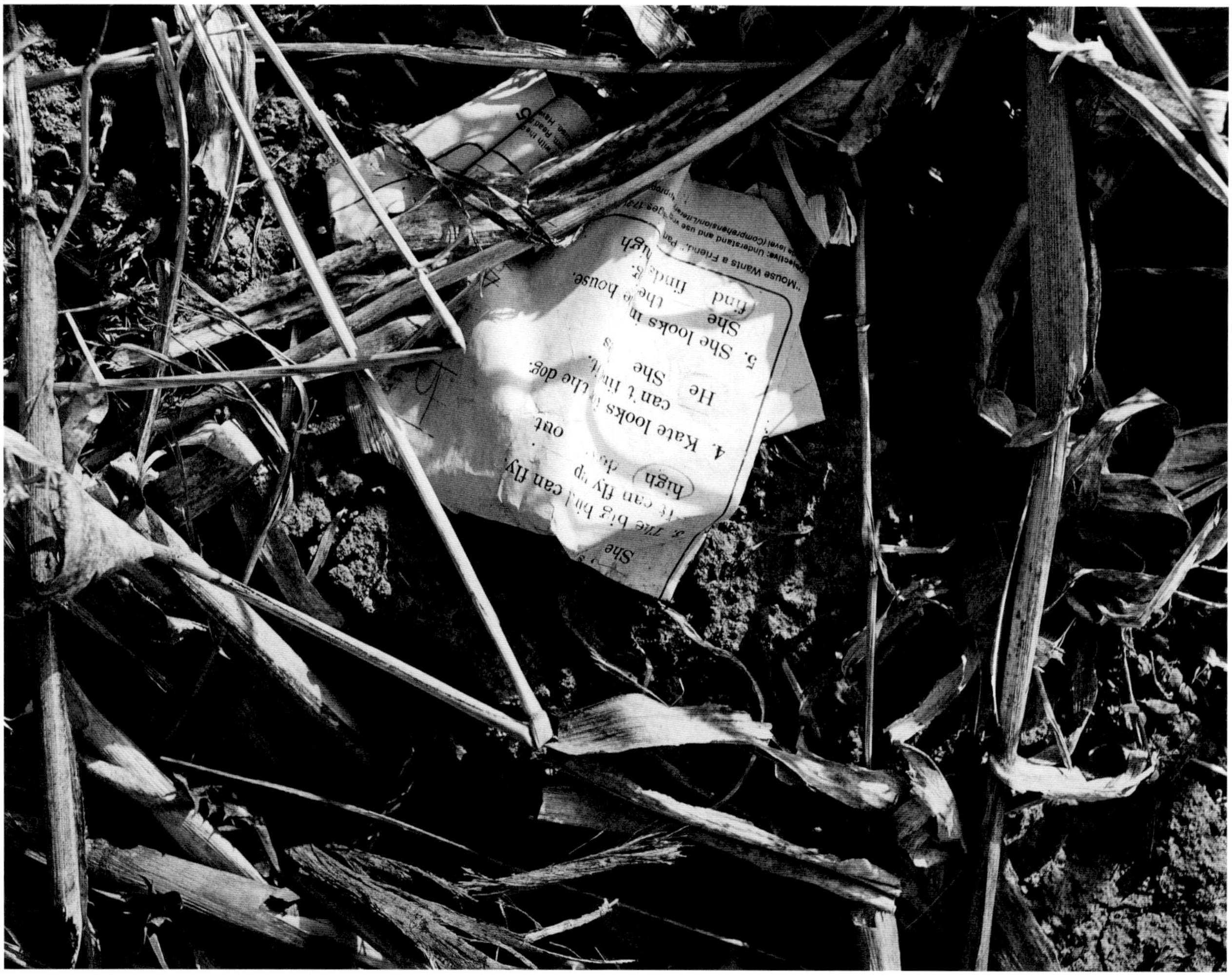

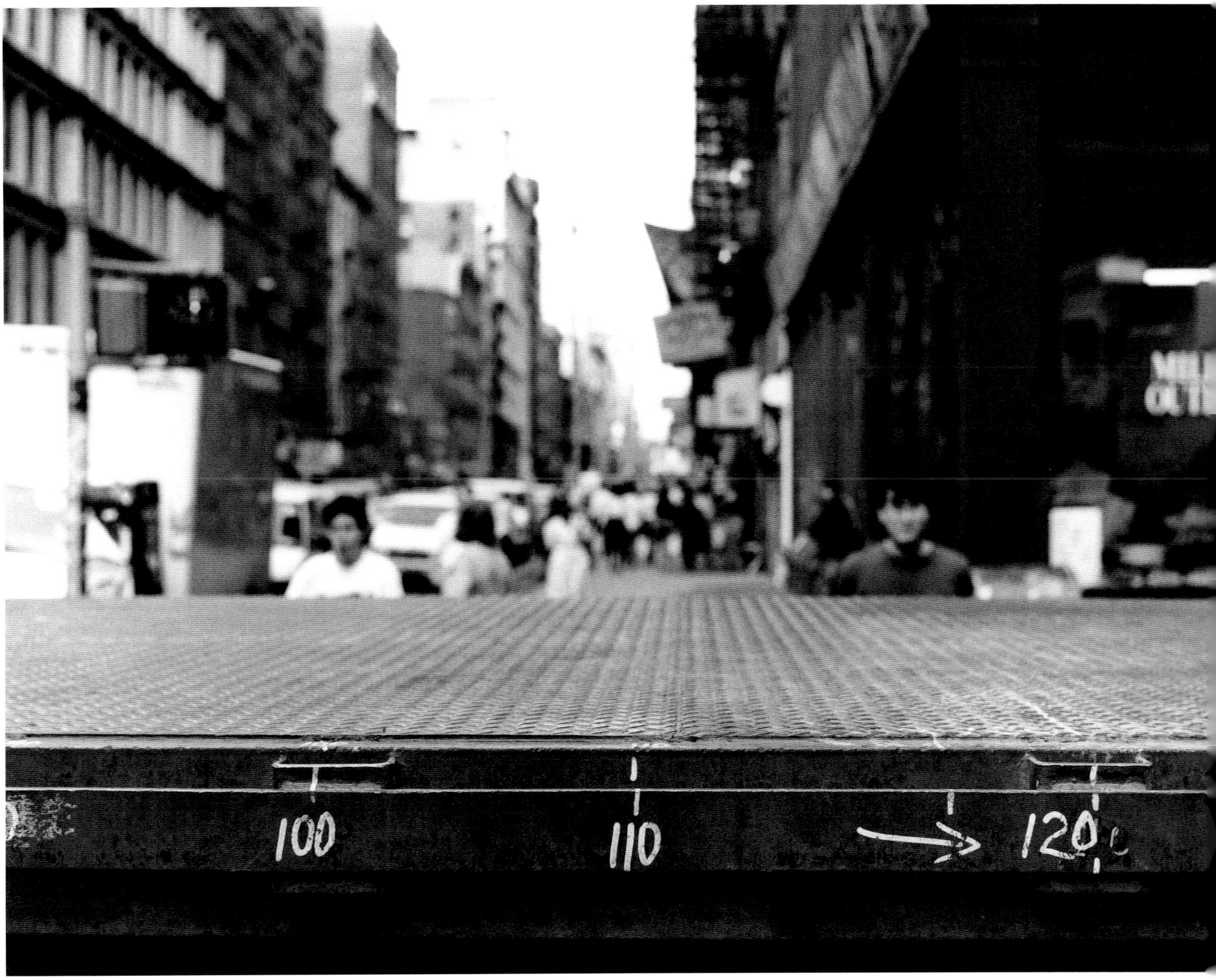
100
110
120

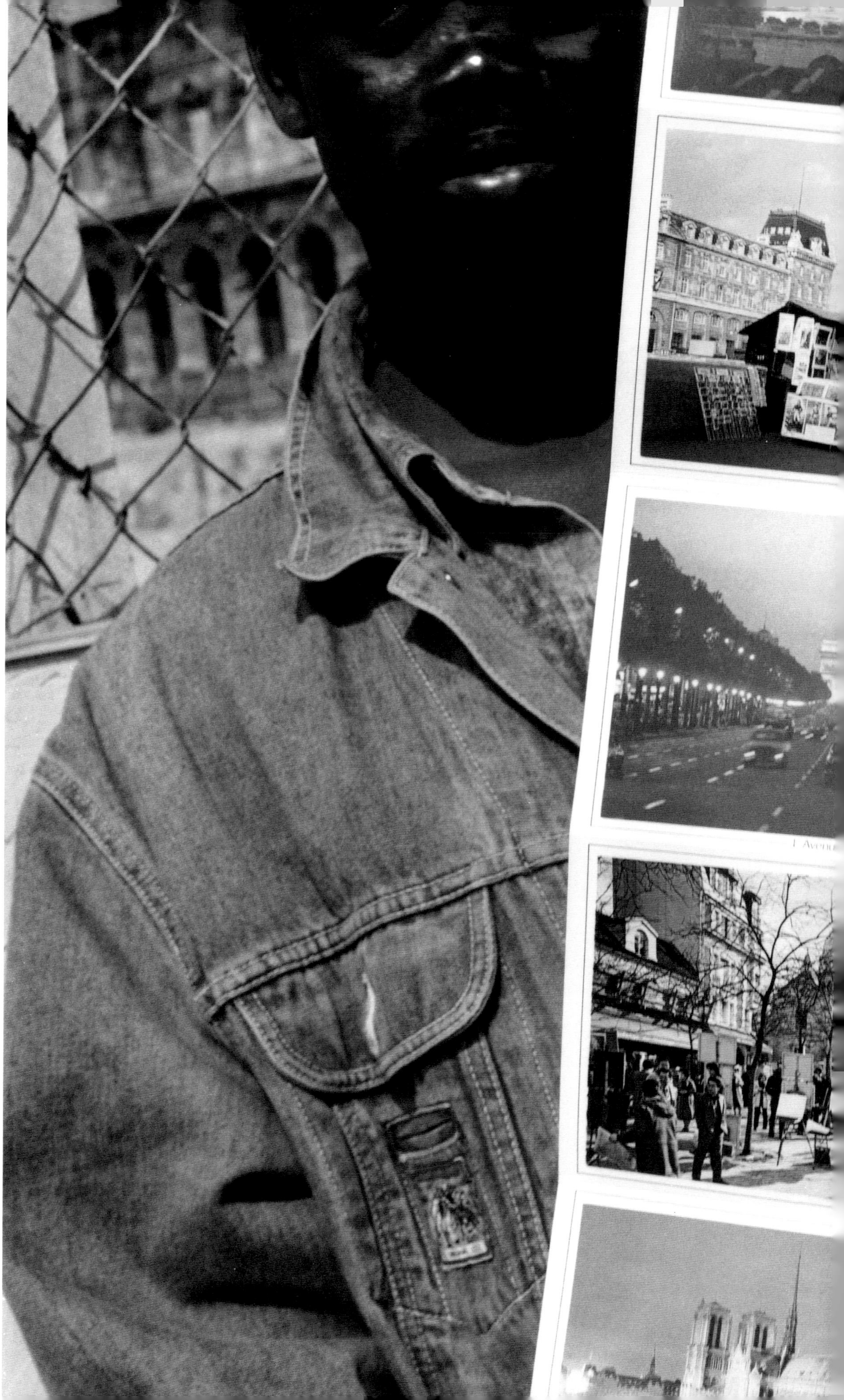

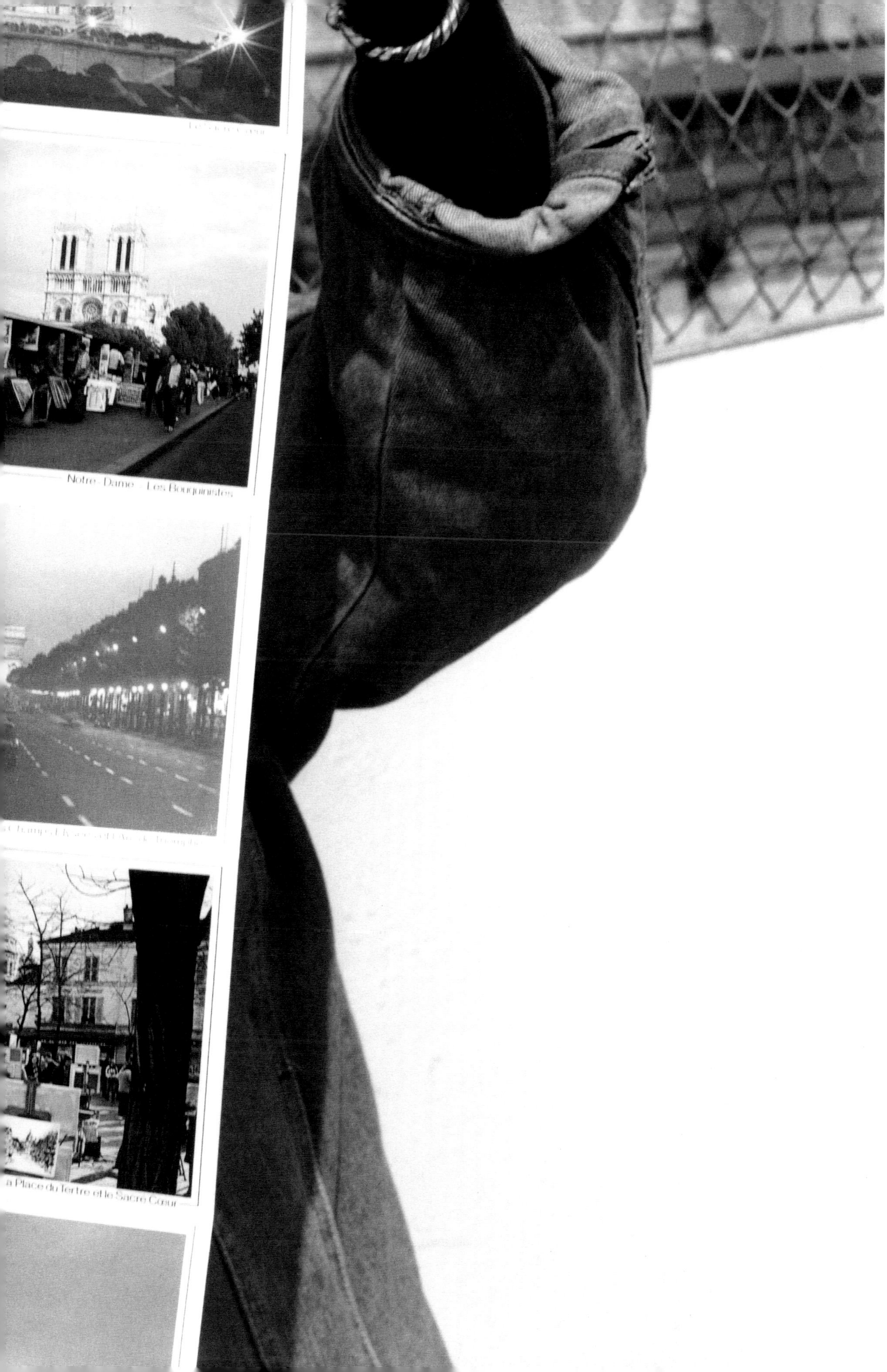
Notre-Dame – Les Bouquinistes
a Place du Tertre et le Sacré Cœur

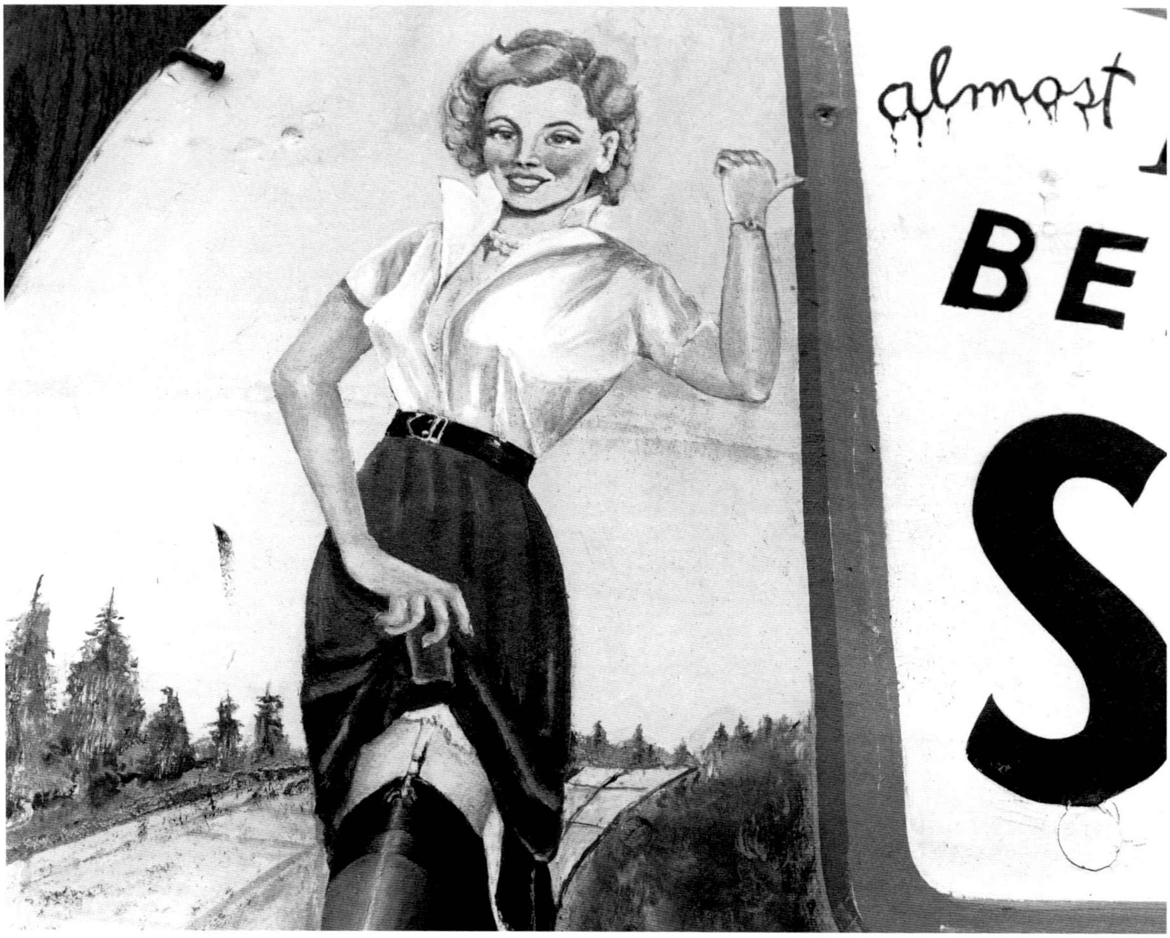
almost
BE
S

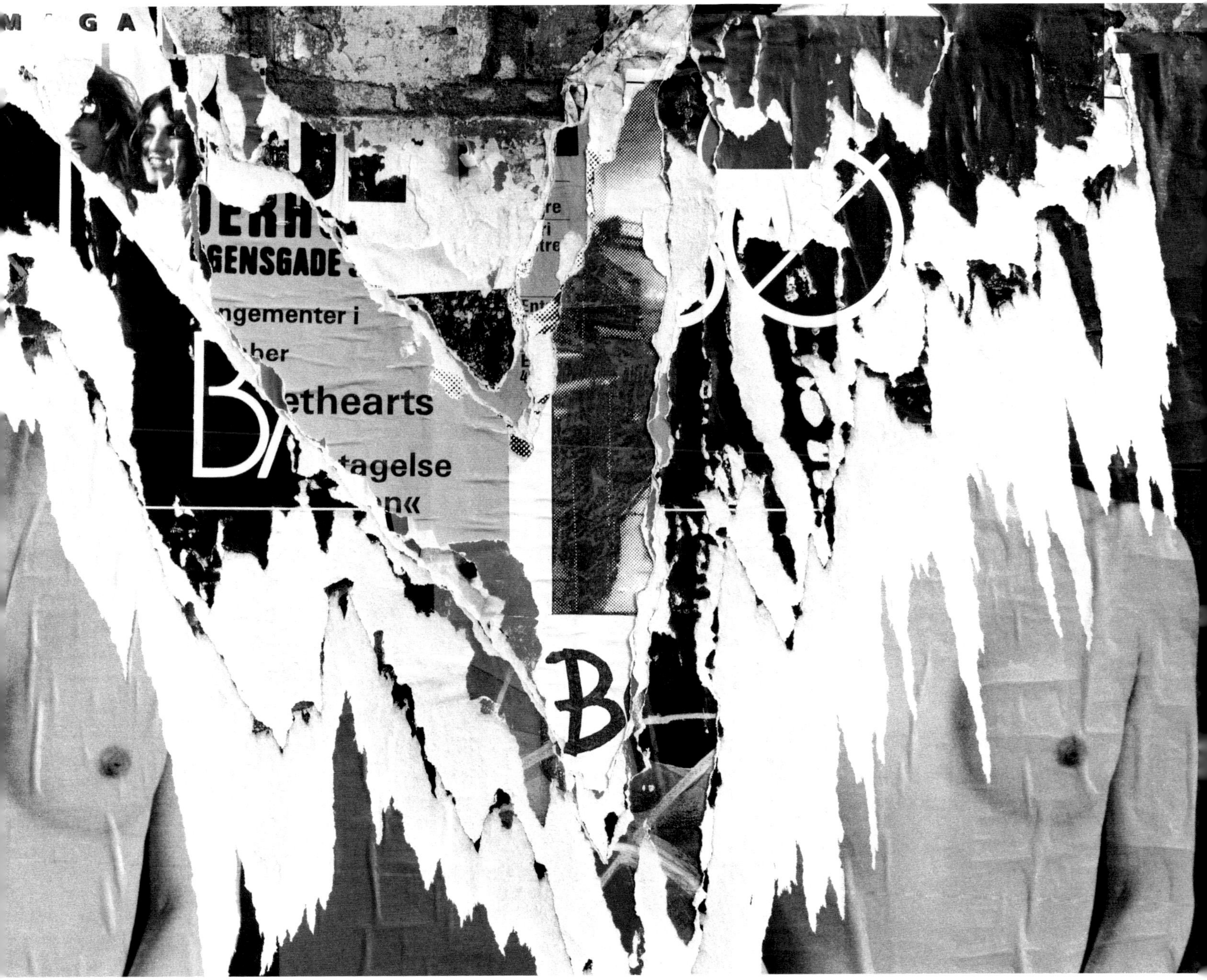
GENSGADE
ngementer i
ber
ethearts
tagelse
n«
B

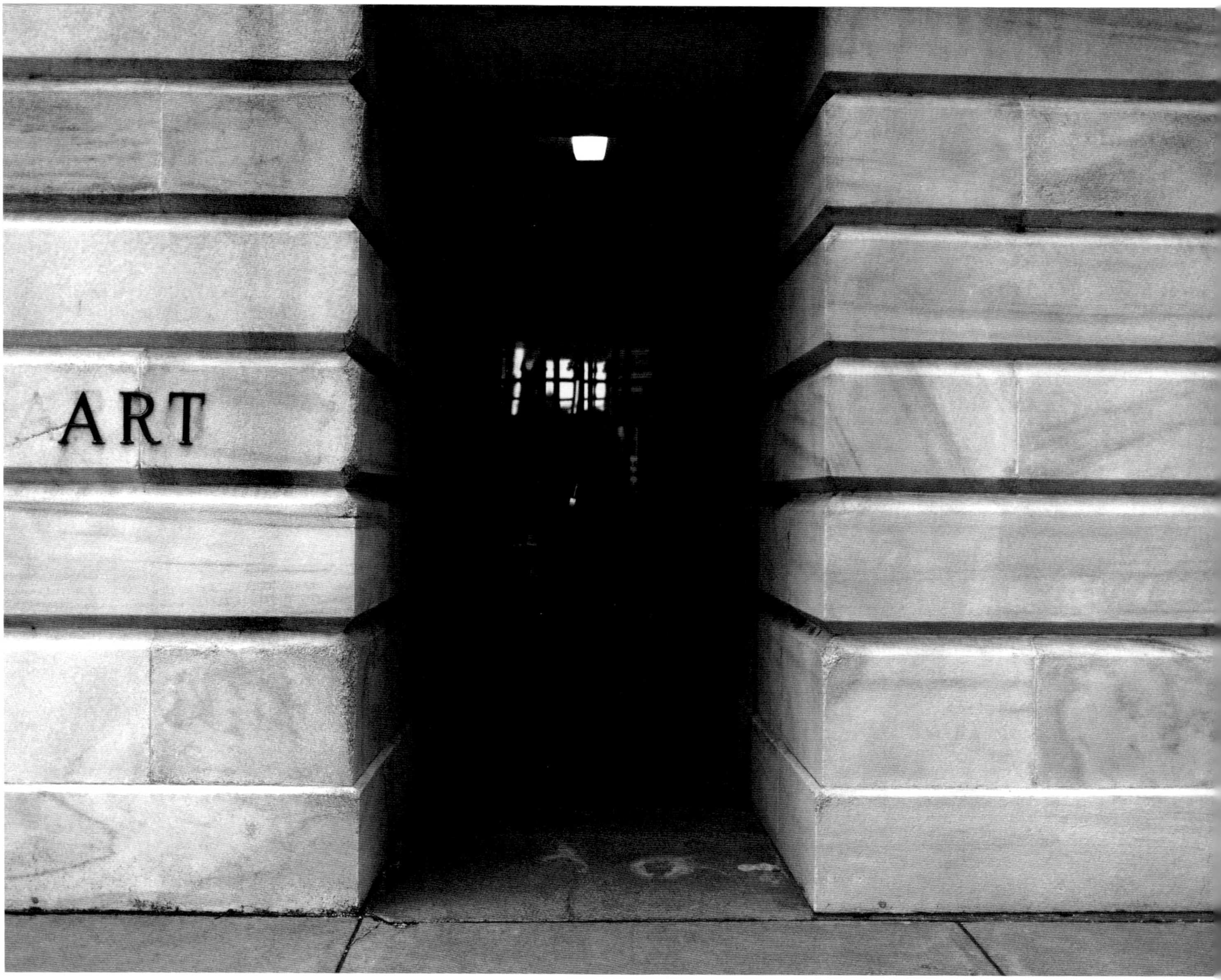
ART

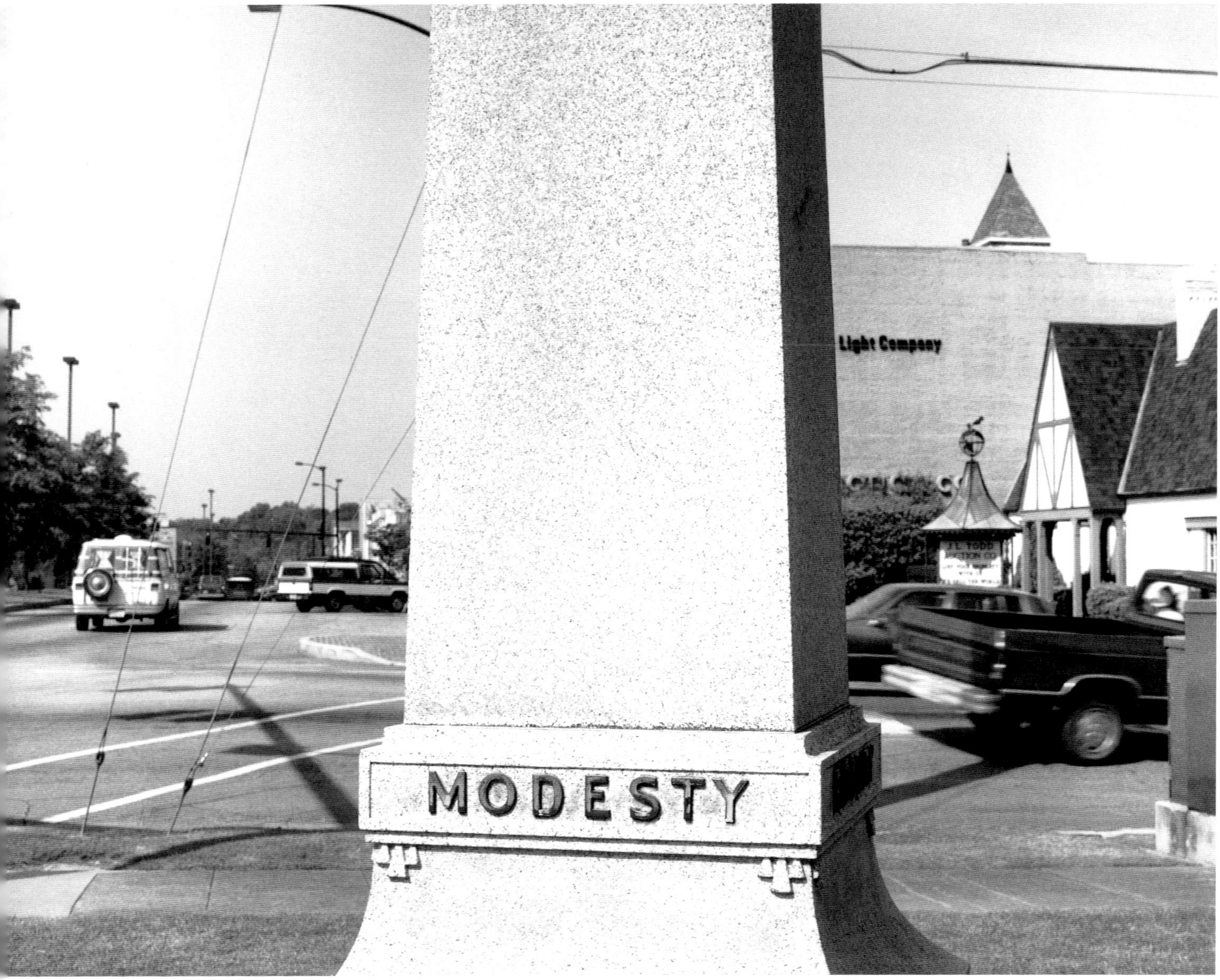
MODESTY
Light Company

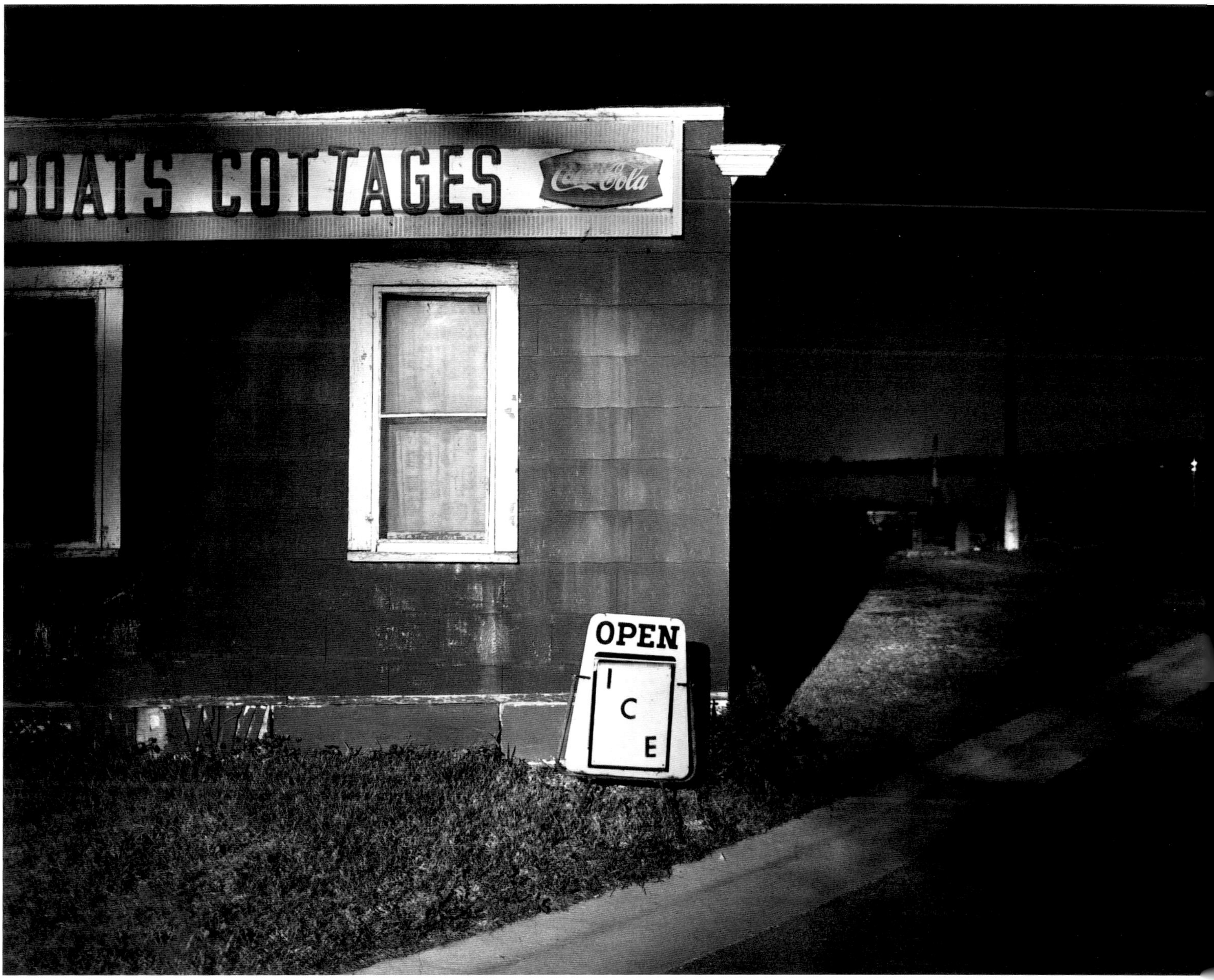
BOATS COTTAGES
Coca-Cola
OPEN
I C E

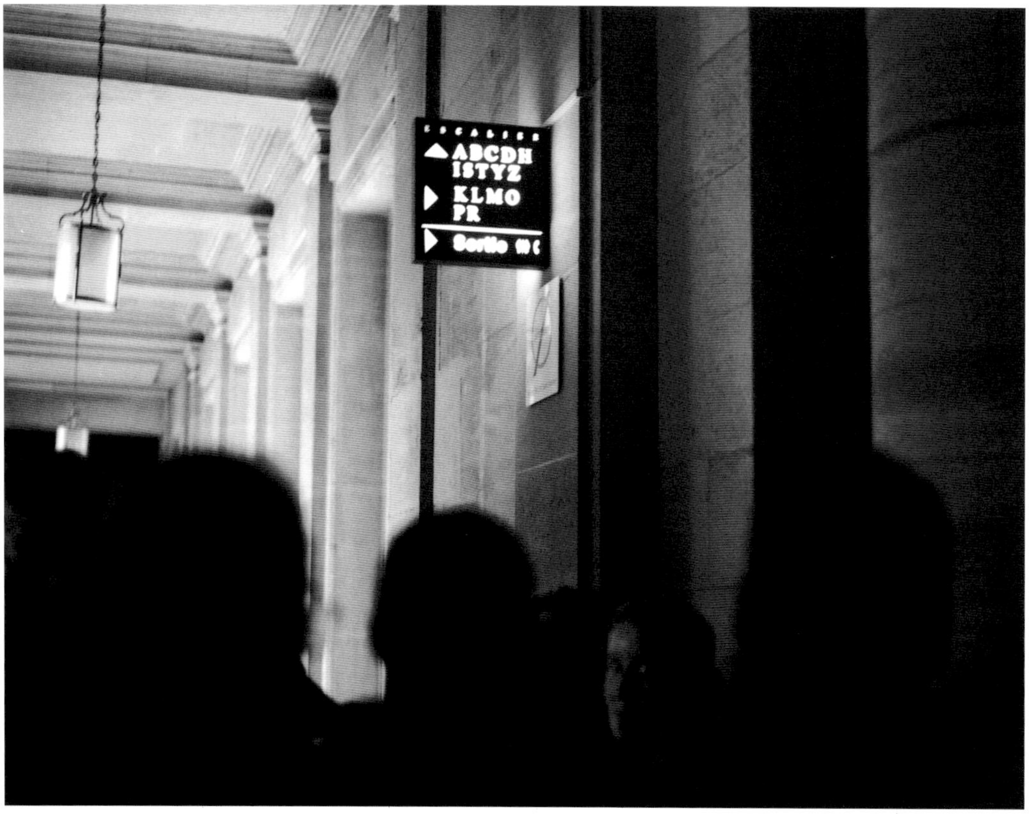
ABCDH
ISTYZ
KLMO
PR
Sortie

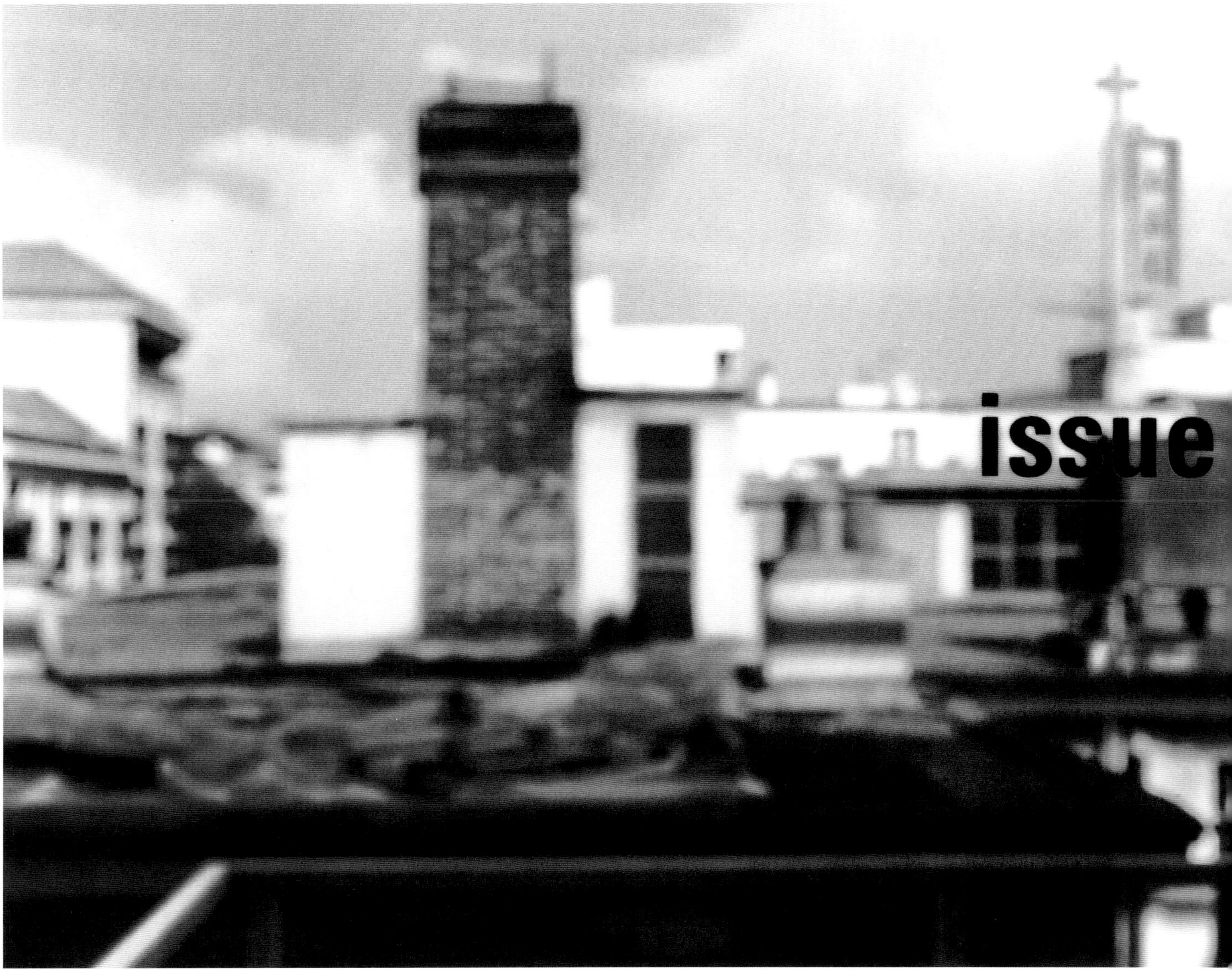

issue

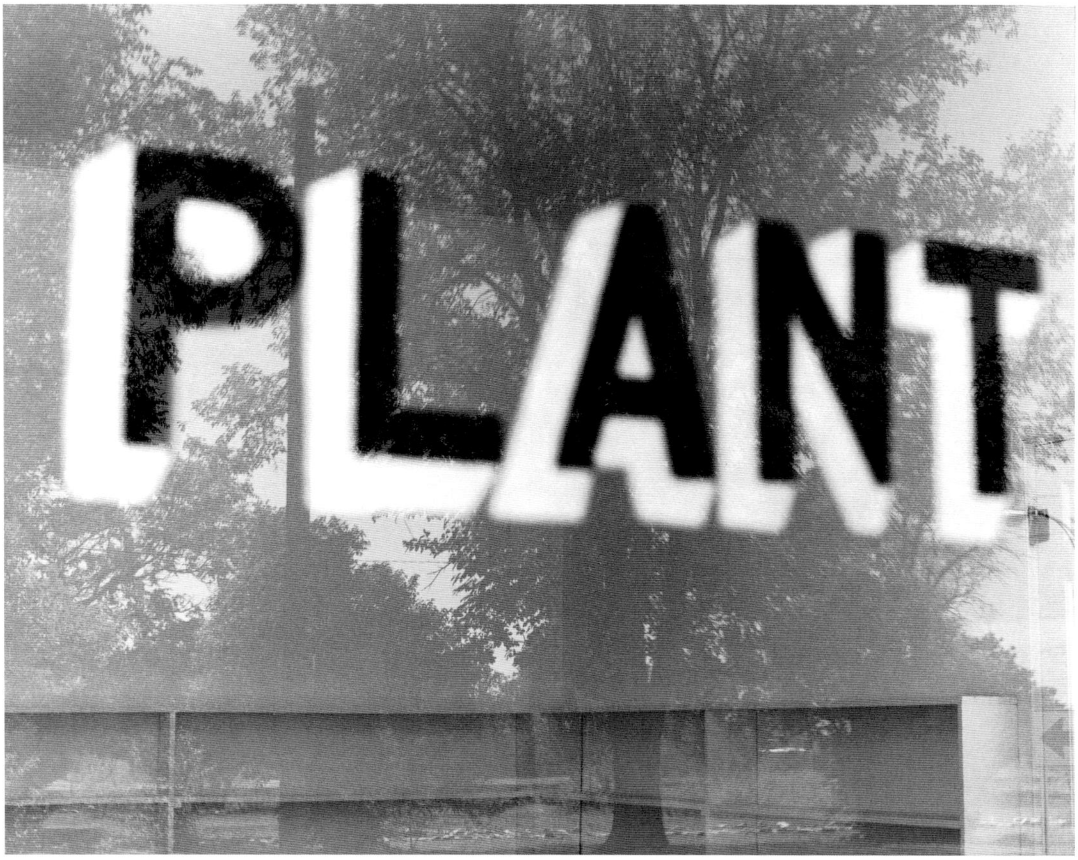
PLANT

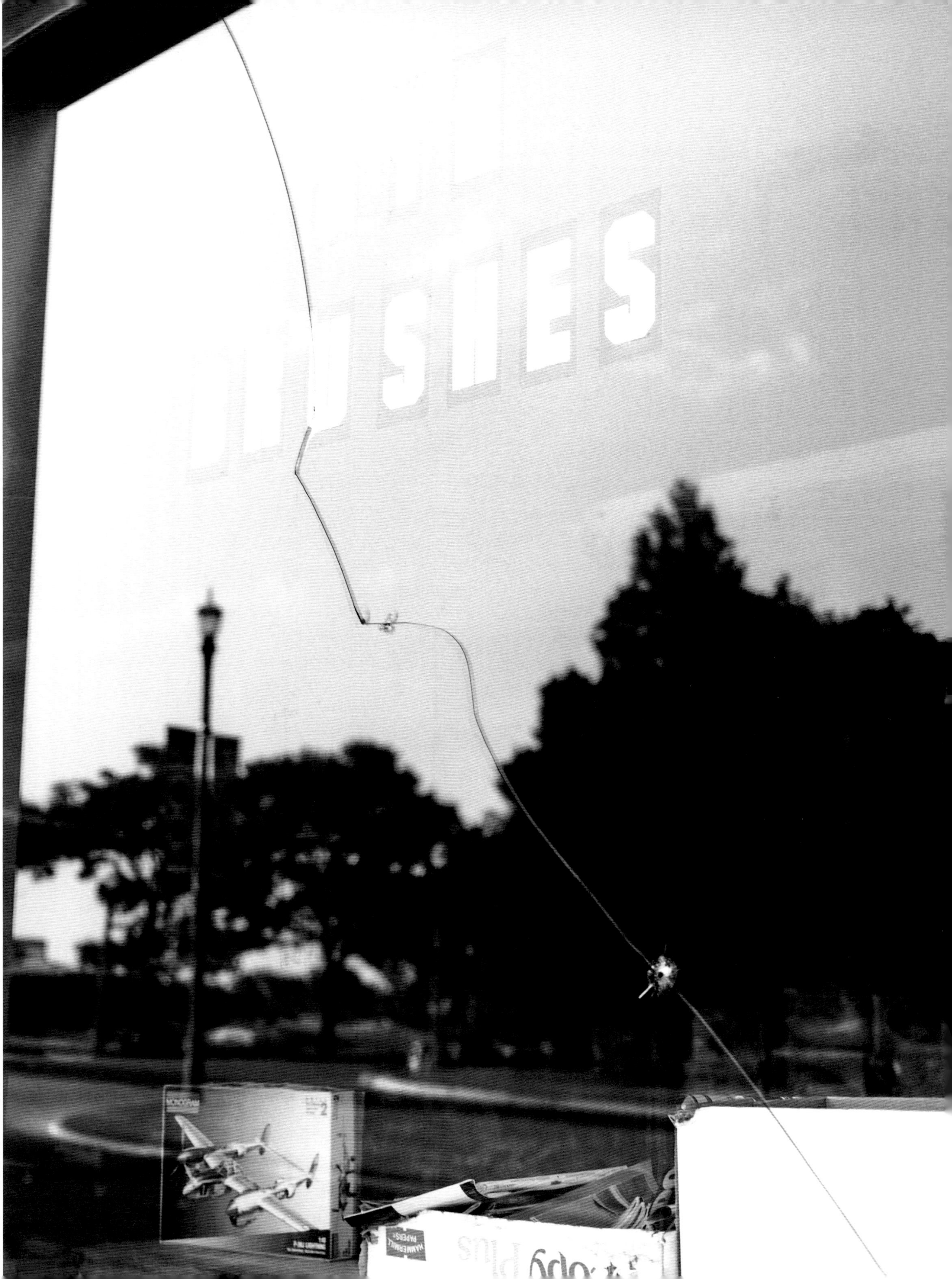

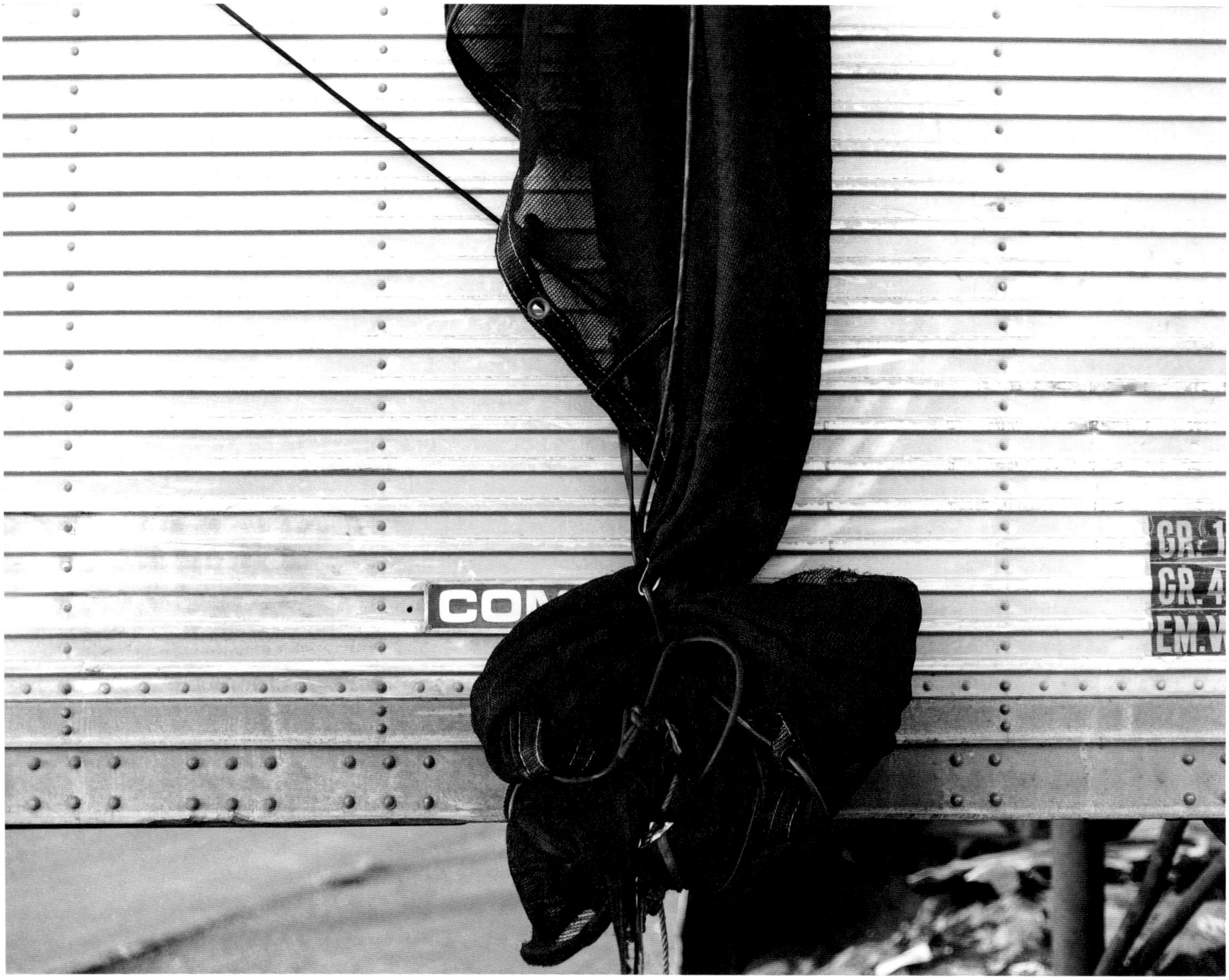
CON

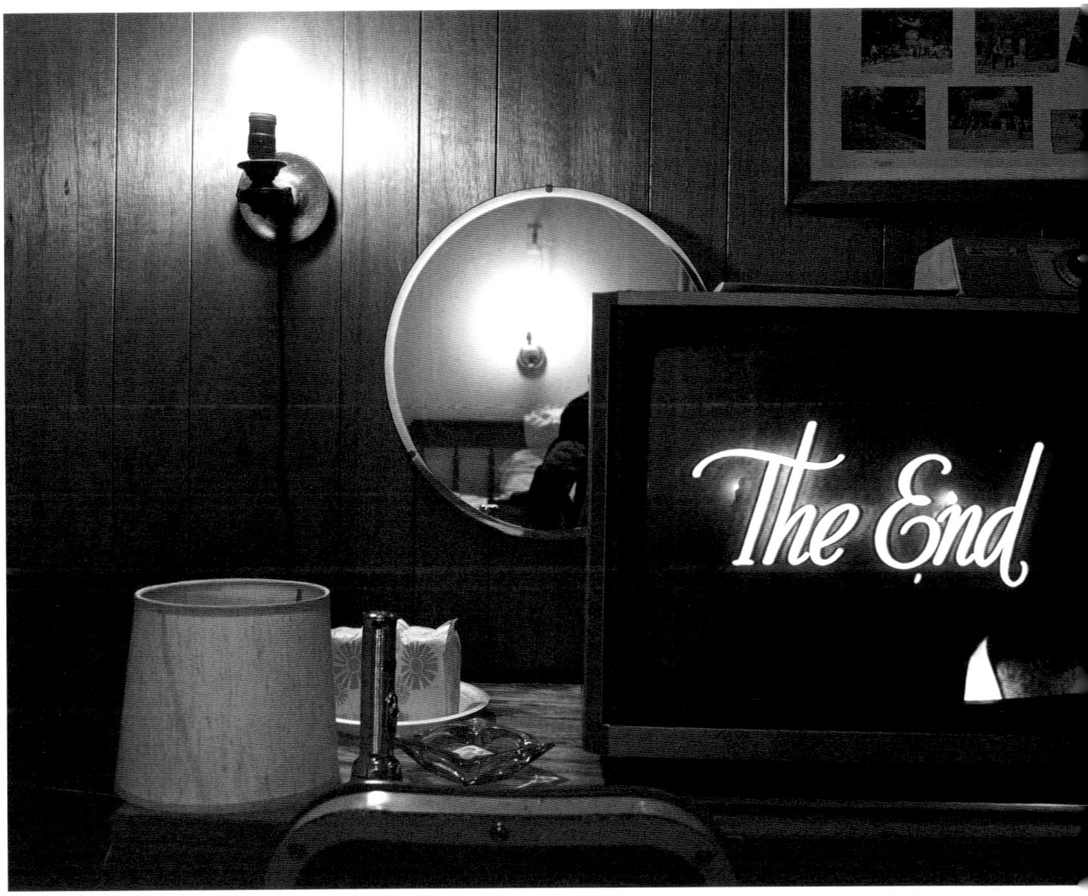
The End

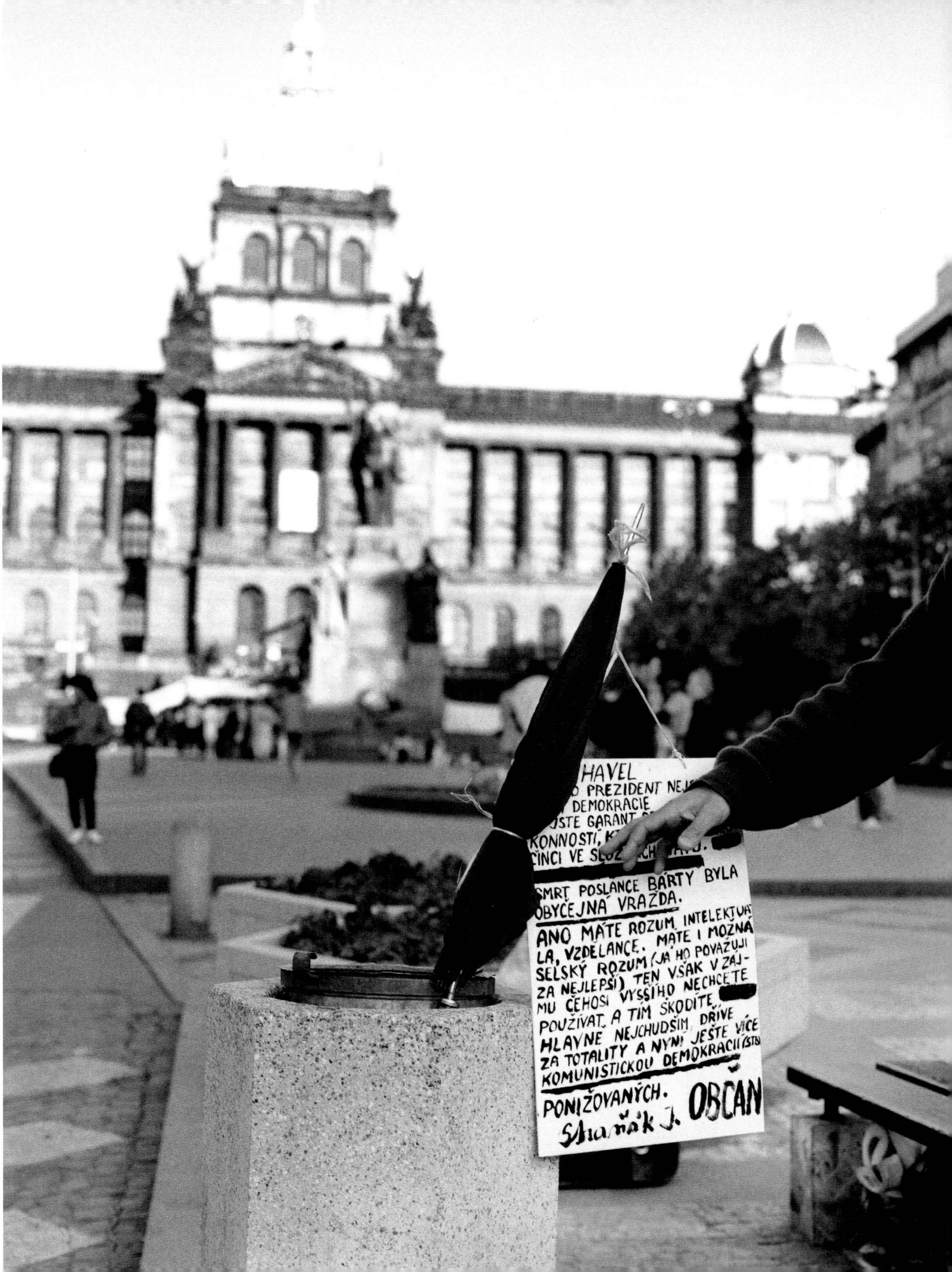
HAVEL
PREZIDENT
DEMOKRACIE
GARANT
KONNOSTÍ,
ČINCI VE
[redacted]
SMRT POSLANCE BÁRTY BYLA
OBYČEJNÁ VRAŽDA.
ANO MÁTE ROZUM INTELEKTUÁ
LA, VZDĚLANCE. MÁTE I MOŽNÁ
SELSKÝ ROZUM (JÁ HO POVAŽUJI
ZA NEJLEPŠÍ) TEN VŠAK V ZÁJ-
MU ČEHOSI VYŠŠÍHO NECHCETE [redacted]
POUŽÍVAT A TÍM ŠKODÍTE,
HLAVNĚ NEJCHUDŠÍM, DŘÍVE
ZA TOTALITY A NYNÍ JEŠTĚ VÍCE
KOMUNISTICKOU DEMOKRACIÍ (STB)
PONIŽOVANÝCH.
OBČAN

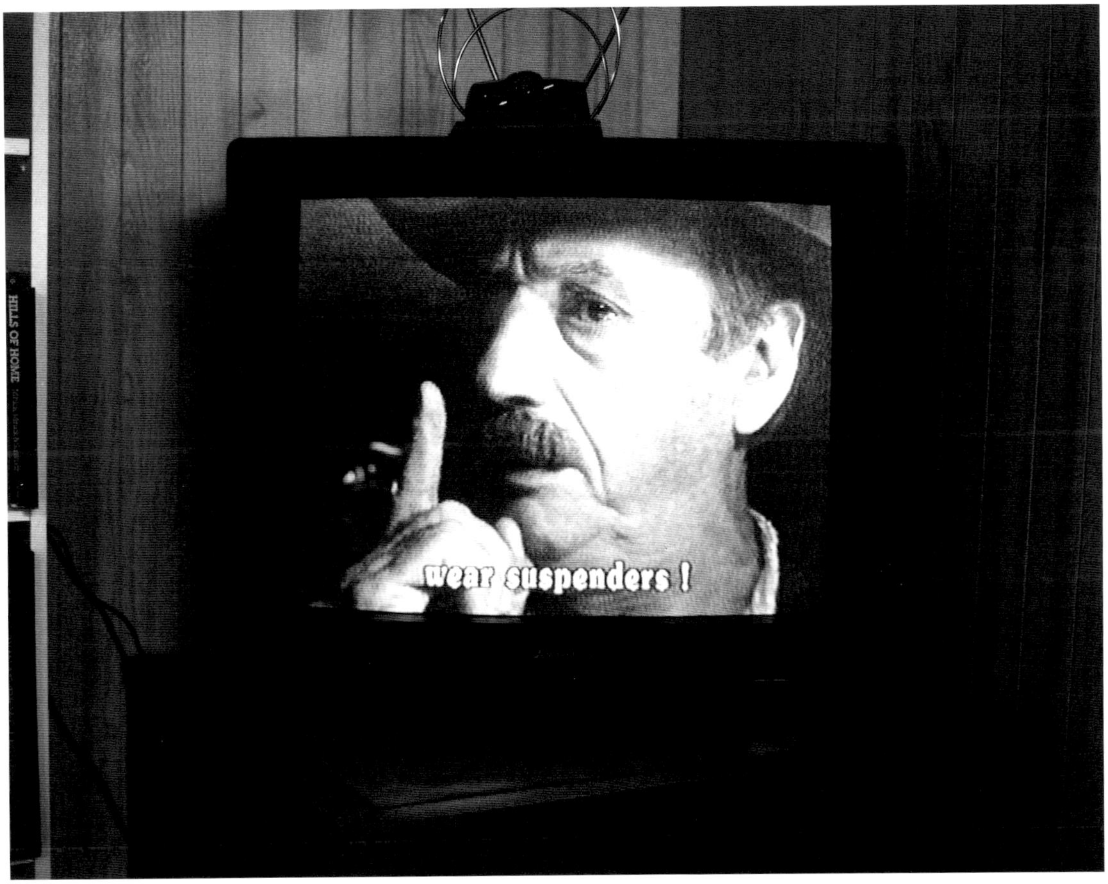
wear suspenders !
HILLS OF HOME

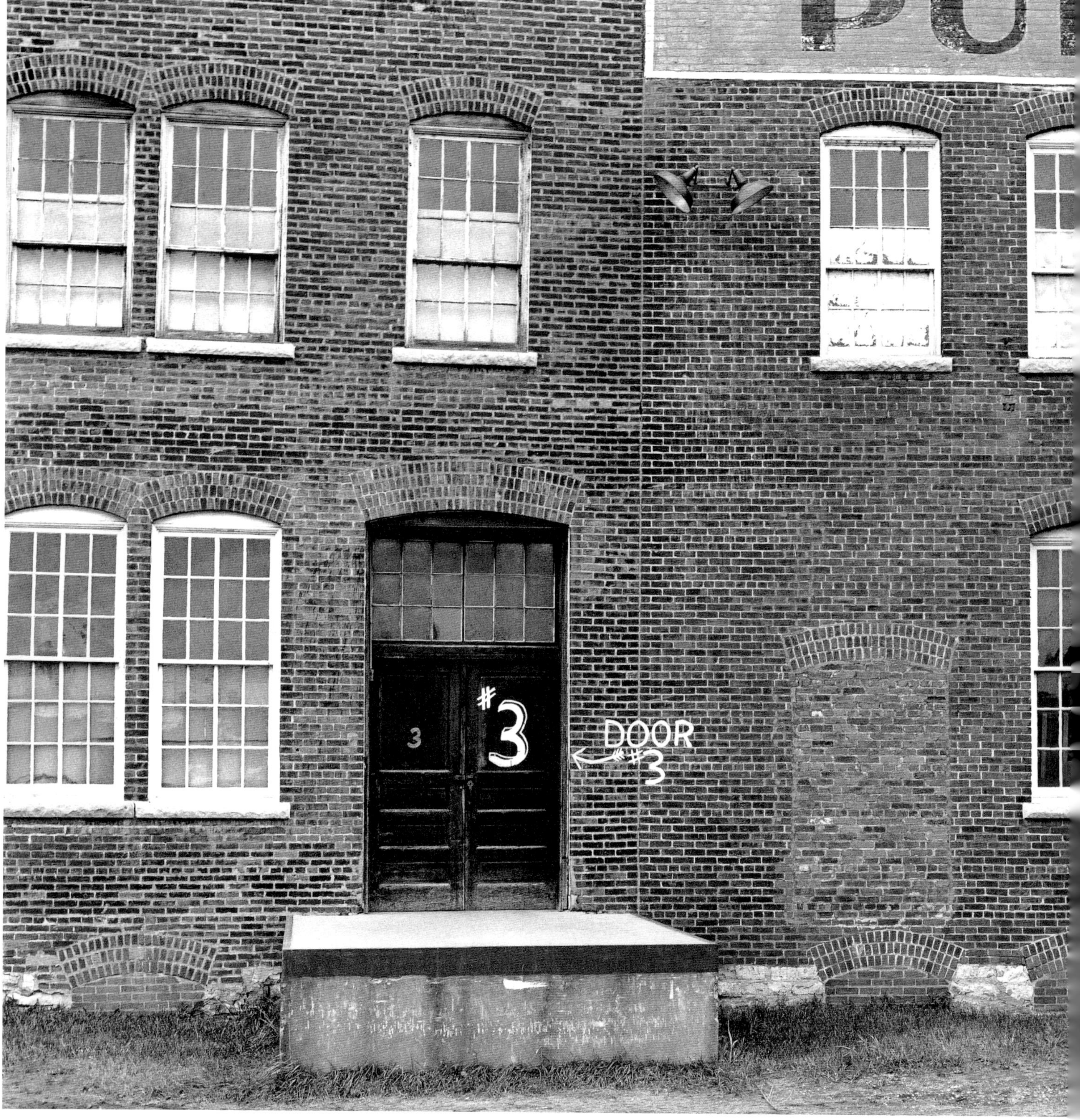
3
#3
DOOR
#3

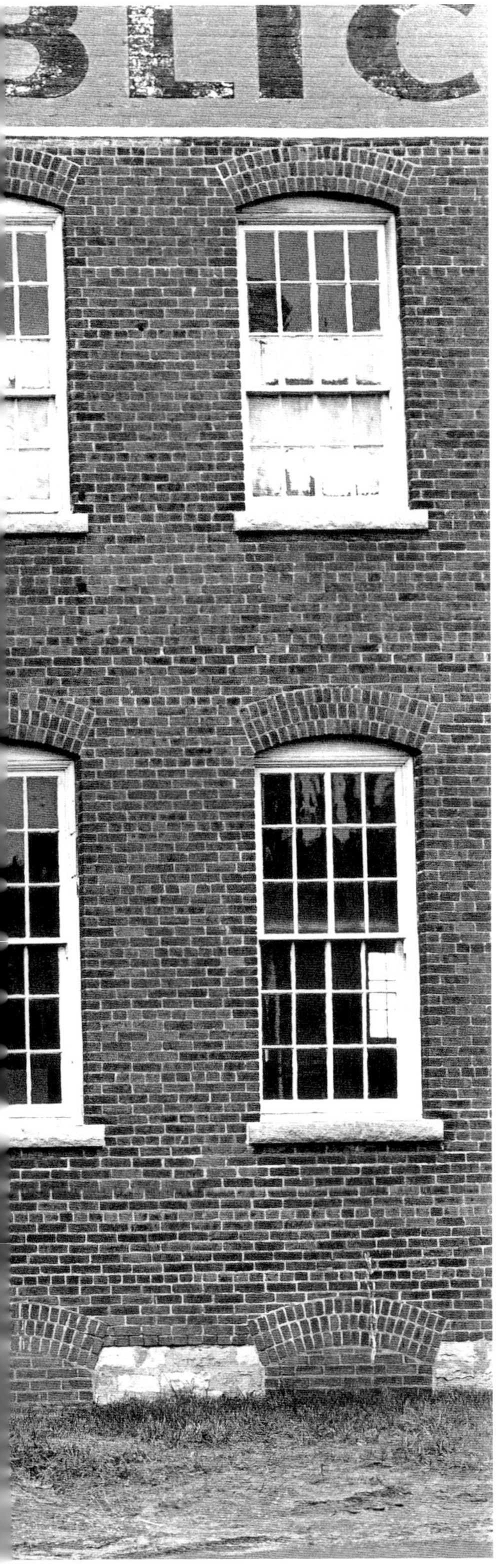
BLIC

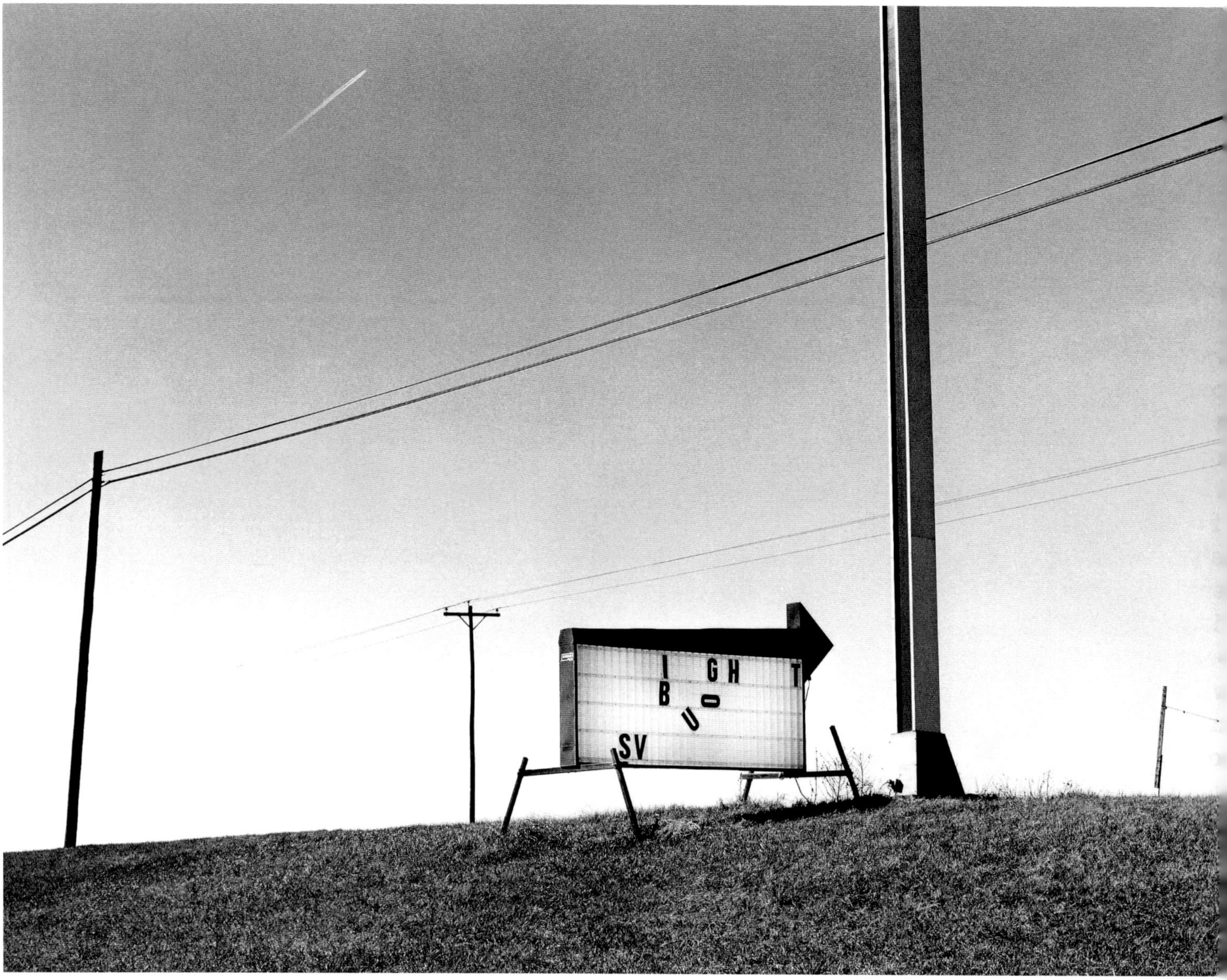
I GH T
B
SV

Along this promenade which joins the ends of days to the ends of nights, indefatigably present, whose length cannot be measured in spite of a suspicion of limits barely offered to our minds, along this promenade where the ends of days joined to the ends of nights succeed to detach themselves to drag miserably adrift of tunnels, from wreck to wreck, castaways of blindness, we perceive the period of life, the period of joys and greatnesses, of despair and of slaveries, within reach of our fixed looks, within reach of compact and fine masses, infinitely sweet to the doubt that follows us along, we perceive objects. By dint of going from sea to mountain the caress is finally torn apart like the wave, henceforth dwells therein the secret of certitude. Imperceptibly profound are the perspectives of this rent, for it calls forth sorrow, its constant companion, and it is only around it, in the flowing circles caused by a stone in clear weather of water and moon, — or by the eddies of a train launched at full speed in the sky, — that life no longer seeks its wherefore and resigns itself to its combustion without shadow nor after-taste. It is not so much the reality of matter and its problematic solidity, as its representation of landmarks to designate space, making us conscious through it of time and our own existence, which attaches the thing of representative form to our mental life. Submarine views, stones of clouds, flights of sharks by waves of applause, retinas of veils, auroras of crustaceans in glass, tables of direction, watches of lightning, crumpled papers that trouble the stars and the thousand feathers of resentment, all that which awakens tenderness out of all reason, unstable flames, sisters of love (the very indifference we often show towards them is the guarantee of a great peace, certitude), from childhood until death do you people this ocean which you accompany with your supreme silence, the feeling which selects you according to the indestructible appearances and the infinitely varying forms of the laws of nature. Things to touch, to eat, to crunch, to apply to the eye, to the skin, to press, to lick, to break, to grind, things to lie, to flee from, to honor, things cold or hot, feminine or masculine, things of day or night which absorb through our pores the greater part of our life, that which expresses itself unnoticed, that which matters because it does not know itself and spends itself without reckoning on the thousand load-stones placed along the edge of the unanimous road, your slumbers fixed in a case of butterflies have put the diamond under all the aspects of the earth, in our childhoods lost inside of ourselves and unspeakably loaded with dreams like the geological layers that serve us as bed sheets.

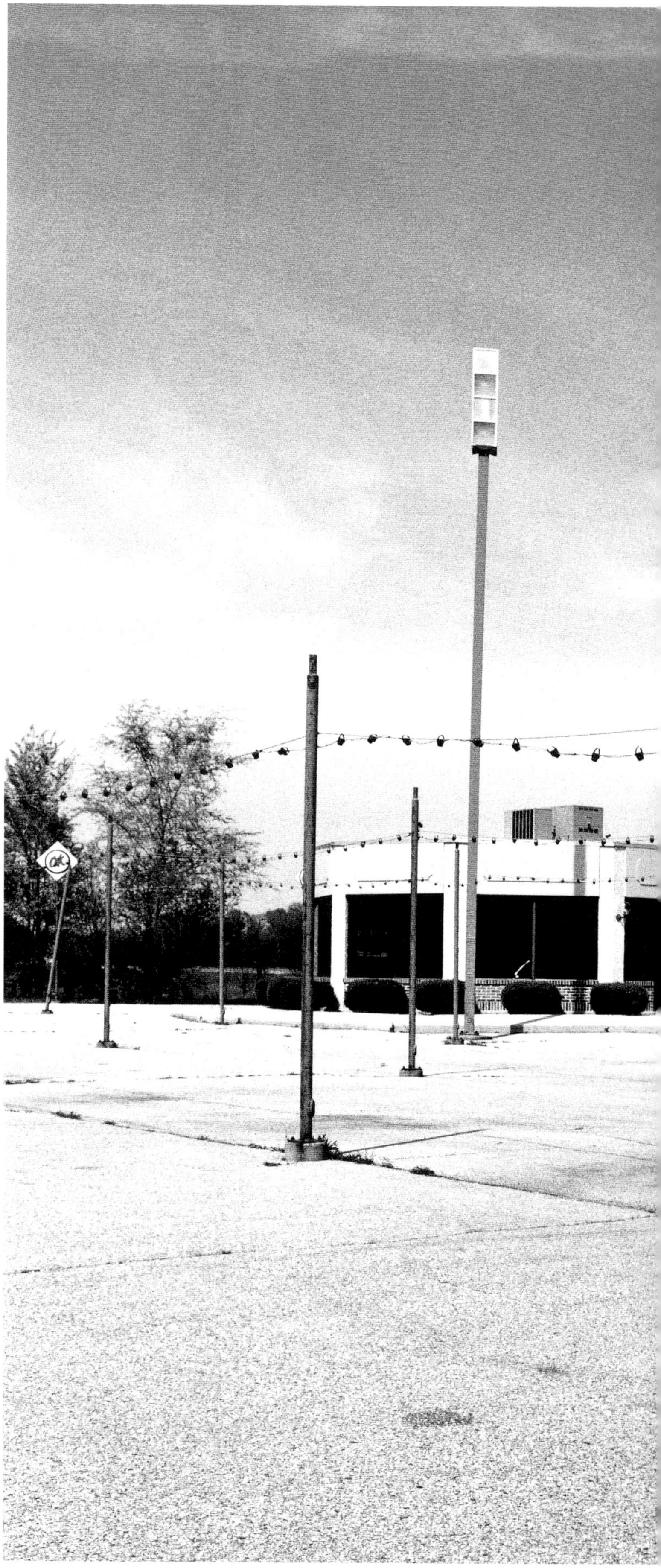

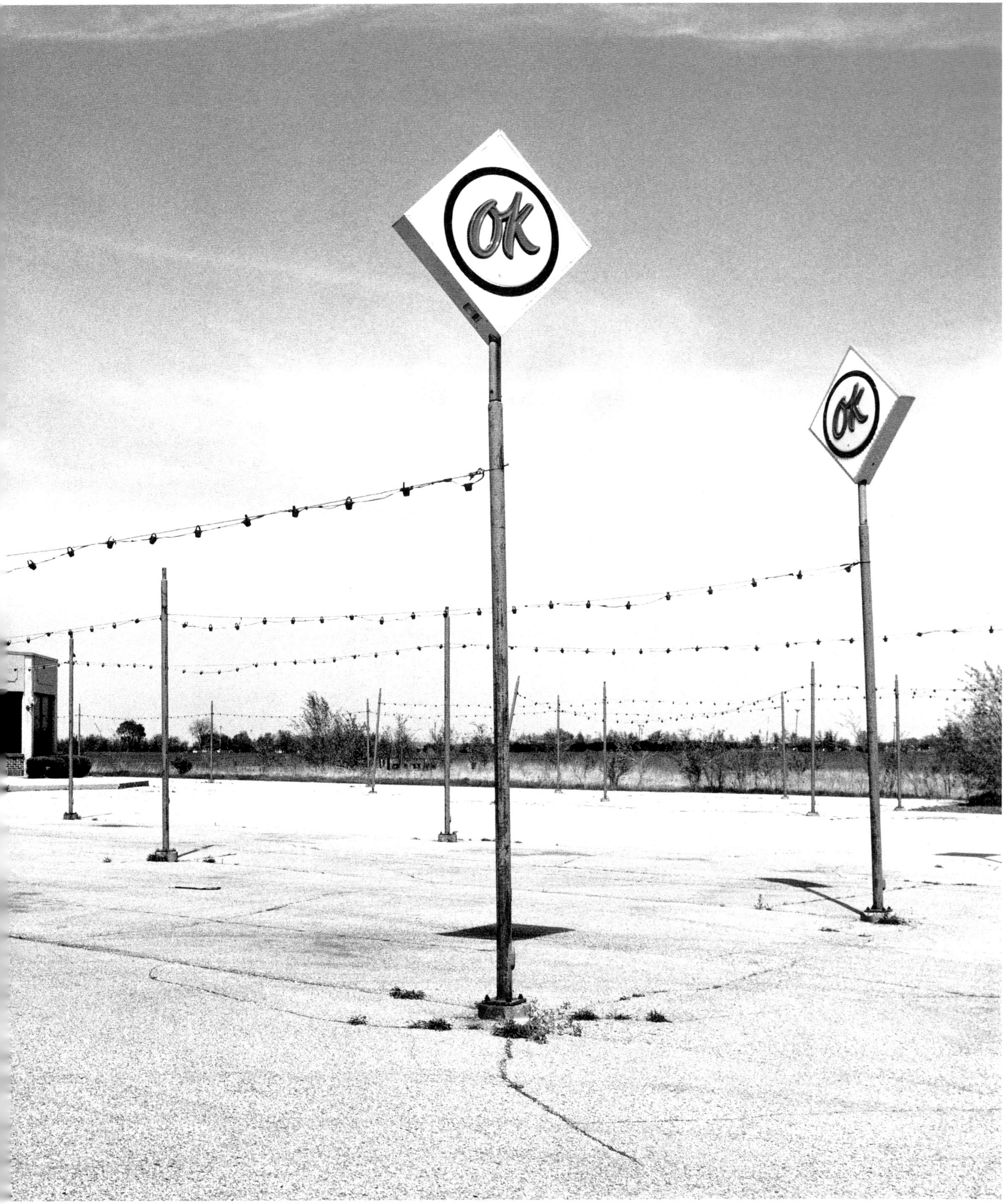
OK
OK

BENEFACTOR
FOUNDERS
ANNA H. WILSTACH
WILLIAM L. ELKINS
JOHN G. JOHNSON
GEORGE W. ELKINS
OHN H. McFADDEN
LES E. MASTBAUM
ADELINE WILLIAMS
HARVEY
AND LISA NORRIS
LOUISE STEVENS
UEL H. KRESS FOUND

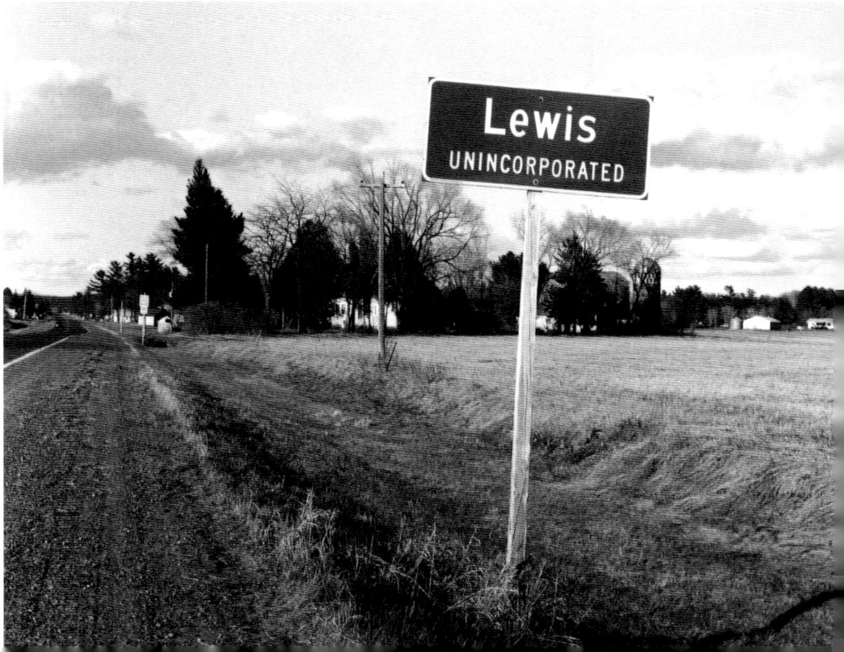
Lewis
UNINCORPORATED

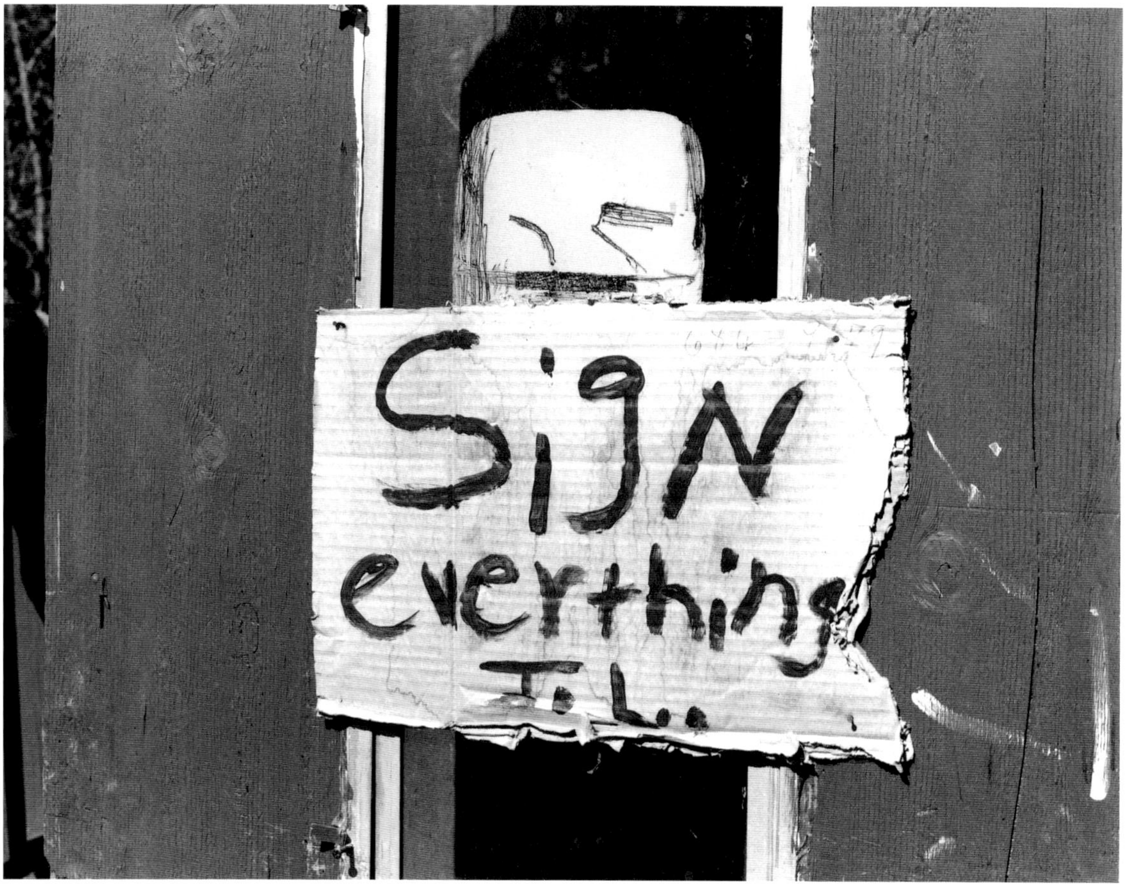
Sign
everthing
J. L.

everything

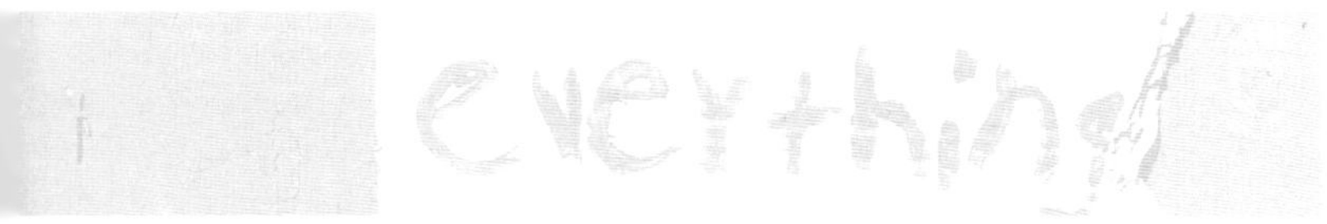

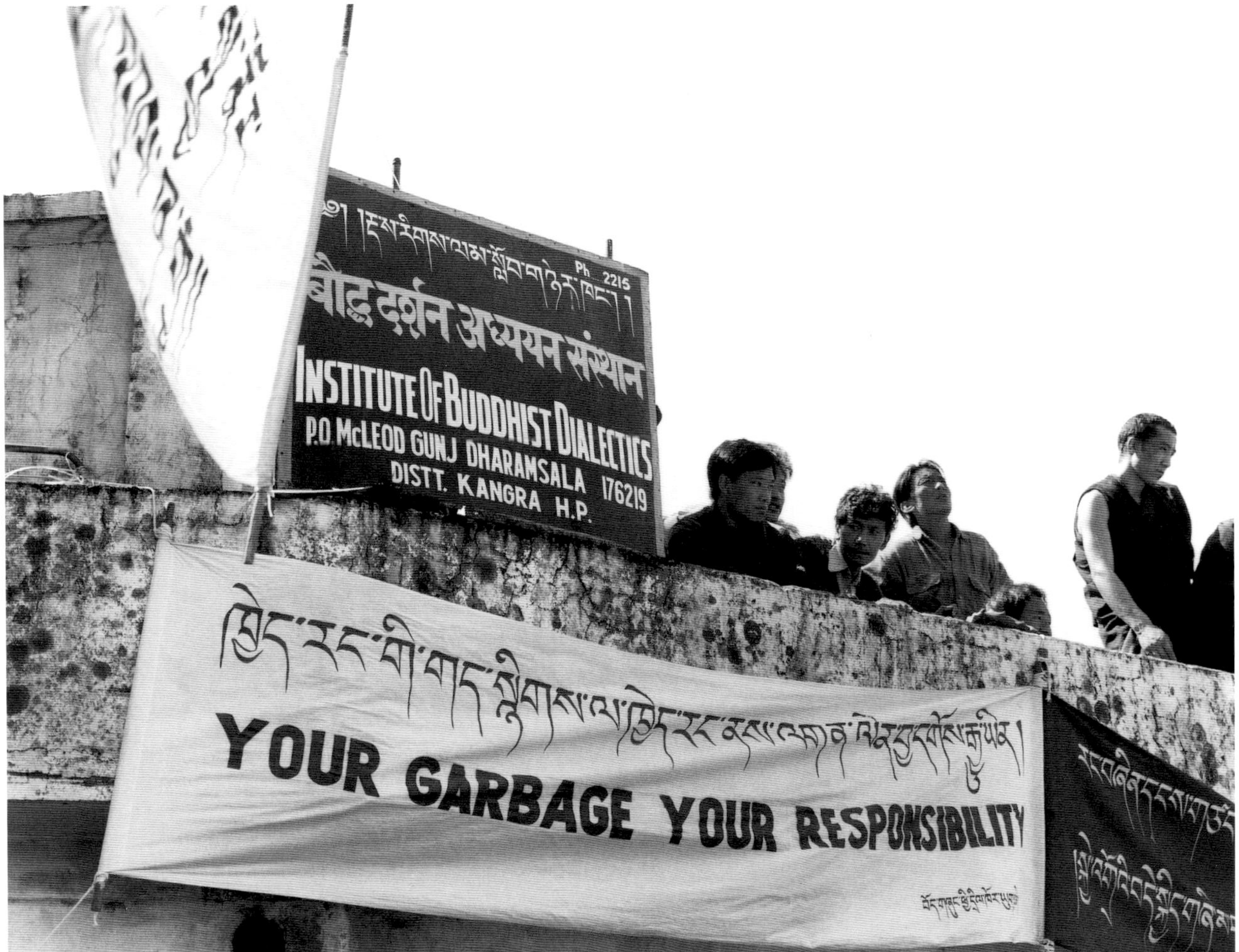
Ph. 2215
बौद्ध दर्शन अध्ययन संस्थान
INSTITUTE OF BUDDHIST DIALECTICS
P.O. McLEOD GUNJ DHARAMSALA 176219
DISTT. KANGRA H.P.
YOUR GARBAGE YOUR RESPONSIBILITY

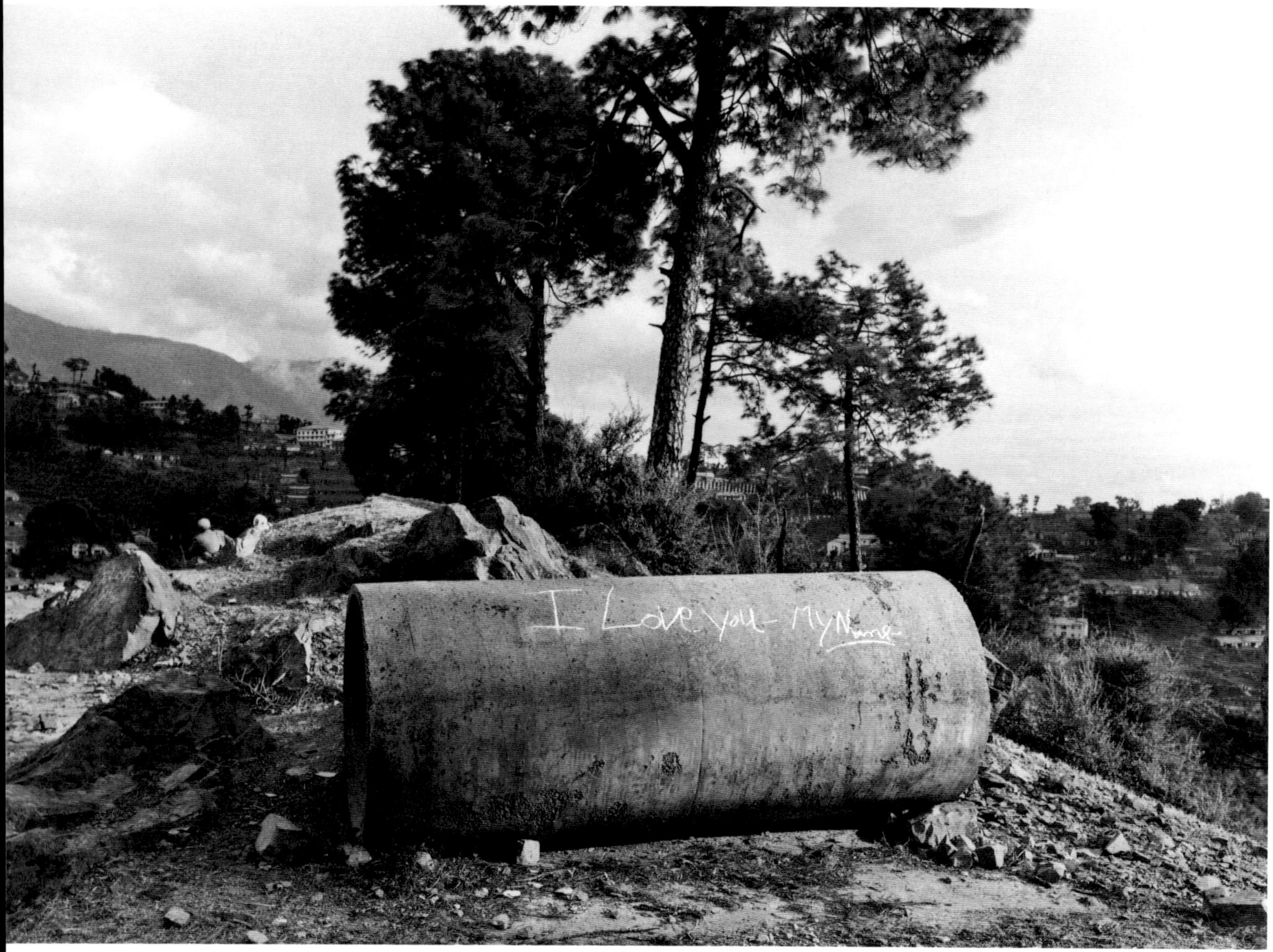
I Love you - My Name

ACKNOWLEDGMENTS

To those who have given so generously to this project their time and expertise in many and various ways: especially Hans Manner-Jakobsen, along with Lars Schwander of the Fotografisk Center, in Copenhagen, who were instrumental in publishing a first, Web-based version of this work; Richard Quinney for his inspired commitment to the process and publishing of fine books; Camilla Kragelund, and Michael William Doyle for their thoughtful insights; Patrick Flynn, and Andy Kraushaar for their considerable design skills; Della Mancuso and all at Capital Offset Company for helping shepherd this work to print; and Sheila Leary and the staff at University of Wisconsin Press for attending to the important details of distribution.

To Arvind Garg, Ulrike Gauss, Larry Hamlin, Ted Hartwell, James Hugunin, Jørgen Jensen, Carole Kismaric, Janet & Richard Koch, Terry Koch, Jean-Claude Lemagny, Philip Martin, John Hallmark Neff, Michael Putnam, Finn Thrane, Julia van Haaften, Marshall Weber, and Christopher Wilde for their early and unwavering belief in this work; and the many friends and colleagues who have kindly shared their thoughts and ideas, including apatrick, Carol Bjerke, Philip Brookman, Barbara Crane, Malcolm Daniel, Michael Duffy, The Flynstitute, Christian Yde Frostholm, Jack Fulton, Jim Goldberg, Ed Greenstein, Alan Griffiths, Peter Hlavacek, David McLimans, Mindy Oh, Jock Reynolds, David Rhodes, Heide Schwerdtner-Kruse, Rod Slemmons, David Tenenbaum, Ron Wallace, and Max Yela. Heartfelt thanks.

To those who have dreamed and wondered out loud, and remain true fonts of inspiration in this puzzle-game called art, particularly Tristan Tzara for his wide embrace, and Man Ray, in whose book, *Photographs by Man Ray, 105 Works, 1920-1934* (Dover, 1979 reprint of the 1934 edition), Tzara's "When Things Dream" first appeared. Additionally, for allowing use of his incandescent verse, John Ashbery is most gratefully acknowledged.

Not finally, but forever, to Annie, Lars, and Megan helping me to imagine in unimaginable ways. And, over the many years, to Rachel Carson, naturalist, author and advocate for a world where a "sense of wonder" lives in the imaginations of all.

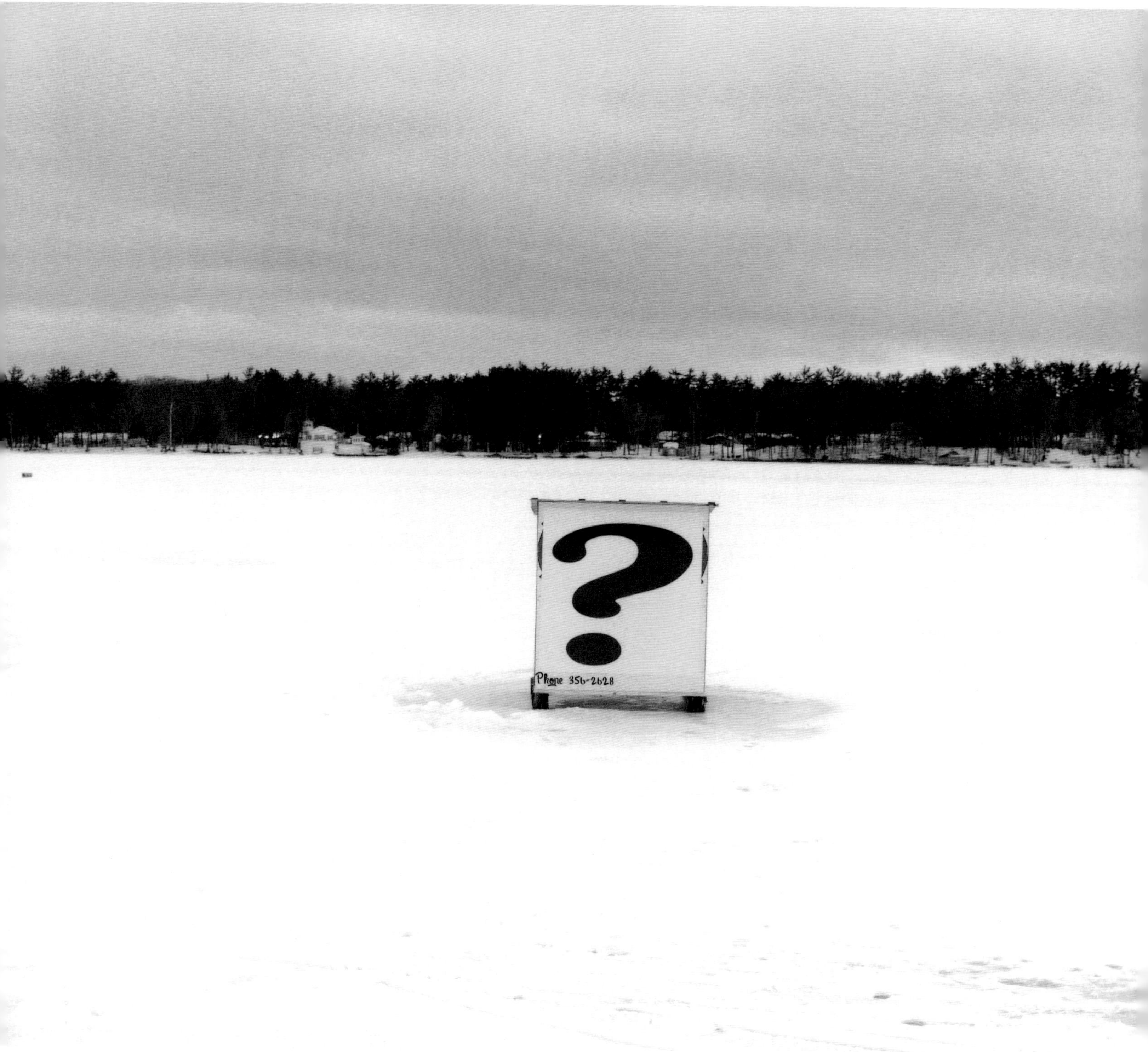
?
Phone 356-2628

Lewis Koch uses photography, text, site-specific installation, video and found objects to call attention to the often unremarked upon elements of everyday life. Over the past thirty years, his work has been shown in garages, on billboards and kiosks, as well as in museums and galleries with solo exhibitions in New York, London, Brussels, Rotterdam, Seoul, San Francisco, Los Angeles, Chicago, Toronto and elsewhere. His photographs and assemblages are in permanent collections throughout the United States, Canada and Europe, including Metropolitan Museum of Art, Whitney Museum of American Art, Staatsgalerie Stuttgart, Maison Européenne de la Photographie–Paris, Museum for Fotokunst–Odense, San Francisco Museum of Modern Art, and Museum of Contemporary Art–Chicago. Grants from the National Endowment for the Arts, Wisconsin Arts Board, and Dane County Cultural Affairs Commission contributed to the making of the photographs, and while artist-in-residence at the Fotografisk Center, Copenhagen, in 2001, the Web project *Touchless Automatic Wonder* was created which became the precedent for this book.

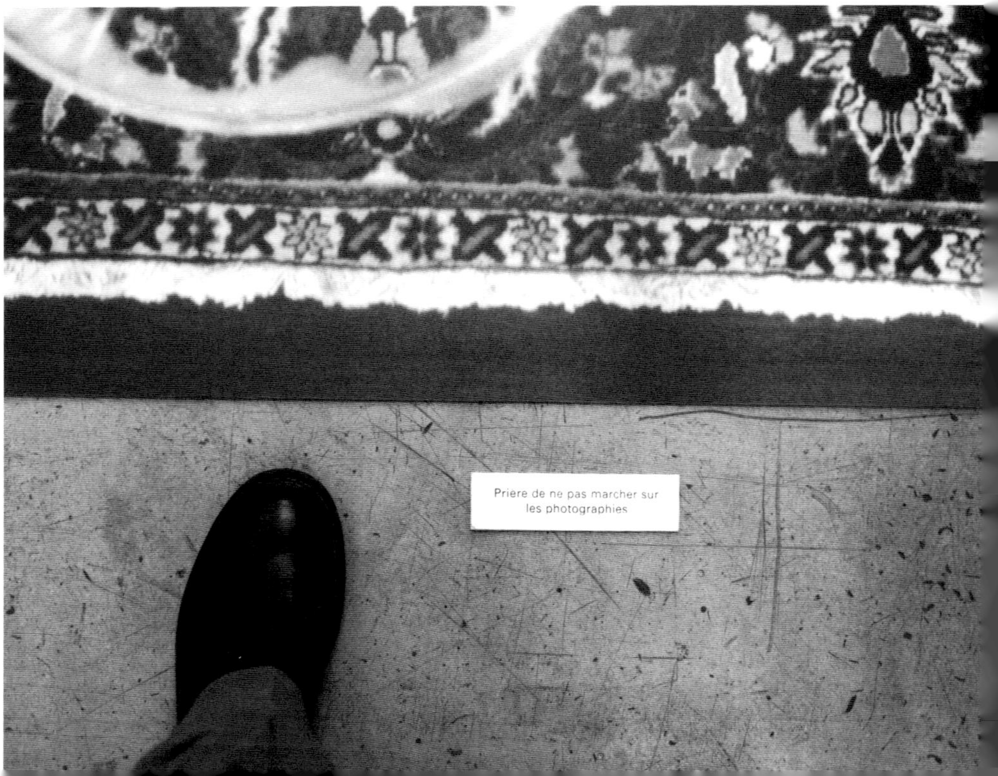
Priere de ne pas marcher sur
les photographies

Published by Borderland Books, Madison, Wisconsin
www.borderlandbooks.net

Photographs, text & book design, Lewis Koch

Duotone scans and printing, Capital Offset Company, Concord, New Hampshire
printed in the United States of America

First Edition of 1500
and Limited Edition of 50 with archival pigment print

Publisher's Cataloging-In-Publication Data

Koch, Lewis, 1949-
Touchless automatic wonder : found text from the real world / photographs by Lewis Koch.

ISBN: 978-0-9815620-4-9

1. Photography, Artistic. 2. Words in art. I. Title.

TR665 .K63 2009
779